Y0-CBF-480

Mentoring
as
COLLABORATION

*Lessons From the Field for
Classroom, School, and District Leaders*

Mary Ann Blank
Cheryl A. Kershaw
Foreword by Robert Eaker

CORWIN PRESS
A SAGE Company

Copyright © 2009 by Corwin Press

All rights reserved. When forms and sample documents are included, their use is authorized only by educators, local school sites, and/or noncommercial or nonprofit entities that have purchased the book. Except for that usage, no part of this book may be reproduced or utilized in any form or by any means, electronic or mechanical, including photocopying, recording, or by any information storage and retrieval system, without permission in writing from the publisher.

For information:

Corwin Press
A SAGE Company
2455 Teller Road
Thousand Oaks, California 91320
www.corwinpress.com

SAGE Publications Ltd.
1 Oliver's Yard
55 City Road
London, EC1Y 1SP
United Kingdom

SAGE Publications India Pvt. Ltd.
B 1/I 1 Mohan Cooperative
Industrial Area
Mathura Road, New Delhi 110 044
India

SAGE Publications Asia-Pacific Pte. Ltd.
33 Pekin Street #02-01
Far East Square
Singapore 048763

Printed in the United States of America.

Library of Congress Cataloging-in-Publication Data

Blank, Mary Ann.
  Mentoring as collaboration: lessons from the field for classroom, school, and district leaders /
Mary Ann Blank, Cheryl A. Kershaw.
     p. cm.
  Includes bibliographical references and index.
  ISBN 978-1-4129-6276-6 (cloth)—ISBN 978-1-4129-6277-3 (pbk.)
  1. Mentoring in education—United States.   2. First year teachers—In-service training—United States.
3. Group work in education—United States.   I. Kershaw, Cheryl.   II. Title.

LB1731.4.B538 2009
371.102—dc22   2008009478

This book is printed on acid-free paper.

08 09 10 11 10 9 8 7 6 5 4 3 2 1

Acquisitions Editor: Carol Chambers Collins
Editorial Assistant: Brett Ory
Production Editor: Appingo Publishing Services
Cover Designer: Scott Van Atta
Graphic Designer: Lisa Riley

Contents

List of Reproducible Figures

List of Figures and Tables

Foreword

What if there were, right now, proven, research-based practices and procedures for effectively mentoring prospective and beginning teachers? And, what if these practices had been successfully implemented in public schools for an extended period of time? In *Mentoring as Collaboration,* Mary Ann Blank and Cheryl Kershaw describe, in specific detail, research-based collaborative structures and strategies that schools and school districts can employ to effectively mentor beginning teachers—strategies they have successfully utilized in real schools with real teachers.

There is virtually unanimous agreement that the way teachers are inducted into the profession is woefully inadequate. Frankly, the old "one semester of student teaching" just doesn't cut it anymore! The world of teaching has become so complex, and the issues facing teachers are so daunting, that teachers—especially new teachers—simply cannot "go it alone." Our profession desperately needs induction and mentoring programs that effectively move teachers from the world of the university to the real world of schools. The authors describe such a program—practices and procedures that are research-based and have been successfully implemented in the K–12 setting.

Mentoring as Collaboration is a remarkable book, not only for the mentoring model that the authors describe but also for the *connections* upon which the mentoring practices and procedures are based. For example, Blank and Kershaw have merged the seemingly disparate worlds of research and practice. The assumptions, practices, and processes in *Mentoring as Collaboration* are research-based. There is no shortage of research documentation. Yet, the mentoring practices are described within the context of real schools and real teachers. Significantly, this makes the book *usable*. The authors have included a treasure of sample forms, documents, guidelines, and examples that readers can readily adapt to their individual situations. In this sense, the mentoring practices that Blank and Kershaw present have been validated both "externally" by the research community and "internally" by the work of public school faculty and staff.

Also, *Mentoring as Collaboration* represents a merger of a number of different research areas—areas of research that are usually written about and implemented separately. The authors have successfully connected the research in such areas as effective teaching, effective schools, leadership, and organizational development—particularly the research related to teaming and creating collaborative cultures.

This book also represents a merger of another kind—a connection between universities and the world of public schools. There has been a cry, literally, for decades for university faculty to "leave their ivory towers" and become *equal* partners with their K–12 counterparts. For the most part, these calls have been in vain. There is simply no longer any reason that universities and public schools should not blend the best of both worlds into a *collaborative partnership.* In *Mentoring as Collaboration,*

Blank and Kershaw take all the excuses off the table. They do not simply describe what a successful university/K–12 partnership can look like—they have successfully practiced such a partnership for years.

Since we know that effective mentoring programs are desperately needed in America's public schools, the question is this: *"Why not now?"* **Mentoring as Collaboration** is a wonderful guide for how to do this work. So, why wait? There is simply no reason to delay implementation of the ideas presented in this terrific book by Mary Ann Blank and Cheryl Kershaw, a book that I predict will become the "gold standard" for mentoring programs in schools throughout North America.

—Robert Eaker

Preface

WHY WE WROTE THIS BOOK—AND WHY EDUCATIONAL LEADERS IN CLASSROOMS, SCHOOLS, AND DISTRICTS NEED IT!

Teacher mentoring has been the cornerstone of a multiyear partnership among The University of Tennessee College of Education, Health, and Human Sciences; Knox County Schools; and the Tennessee State Department of Education to improve teacher quality. Our experiences in collaborating with P–12 school personnel in our partnering district and in others across our state to improve school- and systemwide mentoring is an outgrowth of a Title II Teacher Quality Enhancement Partnership Grant, URBAN IMPACT. What we learned from this collaboration confirmed what we had always intuitively believed about teacher induction and retention. First, effective mentoring directly impacts student achievement. When new teachers are coached by their talented colleagues, they develop effective skills far sooner than do those left to learn to teach on their own. Second, when mentoring provides new teachers with an understanding of the school context and the skills to address the needs of students, it increases the likelihood that they will remain at their school or in the profession. We know from our own experience and from research that teachers enter the profession to "make a difference." They leave when they are not able to do so. Third, school- and system-based mentoring provides talented, nurturing teachers with teacher leadership opportunities that enhance their own professional development as well as their careers. Many high-performing teachers want leadership roles that do not require that they leave their classrooms. Serving as a mentor or a "lead mentor" provides such a career path. Fourth, when school and system administrators understand the link between teacher mentoring and student achievement, they create appropriate structures to support the work of their teacher leaders that transform their school cultures into Professional Learning Communities. Without these structures, mentoring remains a desired activity that is rarely implemented as intended.

We developed the materials in this book for school principals, teacher leaders, school system leaders, and higher education faculty who are responsible for the induction of beginning teachers. During the development phase of our grant-funded Teacher Mentoring and Induction Program (TMIP), we used the materials for intensive professional development sessions with P–12 teachers to establish "Mentor Core Teams" (MCT) in high-need schools. Over the past nine years, we have seen this initial approach expanded to a systemwide program for supporting new teachers in all schools. We have also found that it has enhanced the work of teacher educators in collaborating with school personnel for scaffolding the induction of their teacher preparation students. All teacher educators recognize that placing their preservice candidates in schools with strong school-based mentoring leadership enhances the quality of the teacher preparation experience. We have learned that when university and school leaders work together to improve the induction of new teachers, the quality of teacher preparation and mentoring, as well as of teaching and learning, is strengthened. The "sum" of this collaboration on supporting talented teachers is far greater than any of its parts.

Why is this book important to P–16 educators? First, it provides structures, practices, and real-world examples of how to transform the concept of teacher mentoring and induction from socialization and sporadic coaching to intentional, research-based coaching. Assigning a mentor to every new teacher has long been an established practice that fulfills state-legislated mandates and school system expectations for retaining good teachers. Its link to improving student achievement has not been widely recognized. The insights, practices, and materials in this book will help school leaders transform the historically "hoped for" mentoring process into a systematic and systemic component of improving school and student outcomes. Second, it provides a school-based model that nurtures beginning teachers while developing the capacity of experienced teachers to serve as effective mentors. It includes structures, policies, and practices that have been developed by our partnering teachers and administrators. Third, it also provides structures for strengthening and sustaining teacher induction practices across the school system. The program has generated significant support and interest because of the clear roles, expectations, and experiences for new teachers, mentors, and school leaders. What began as a program for high-need "urban" schools became equally important to principals and teacher leaders in all school contexts in promoting quality mentoring, creating supportive school cultures, and forming collaborative learning communities. Ultimately, our partnership school system decided that every school should have a well-trained Mentor Core Team that not only knew how to coach new teachers but also had the skills and dispositions to tailor their plans to their own unique contexts, to make annual "fine tuning" adjustments as needed, and to document impact on teacher work satisfaction and retention and student achievement.

> " —— **A Comment From the Field** ——
>
> I told you the first year of the grant funding that I would love to participate in the mentoring program, but I hadn't had more than three new teachers in the past ten years. Little did I know that the system would offer a retirement bonus that would entice more than 75 percent of my faculty [t]. What was not a concern for me then is a priority to me today. I never considered the looming impact of my "graying faculty."
>
> *Elementary Principal* "

As teacher educators committed to improving the development of beginning teachers and the school environments in which they learn to teach, we have worked closely with our local school system central office administrators in the design, implementation, and refinement phases of the Teacher Mentoring and Induction Program. Each partner has contributed to every phase of the program's development, and all are responsible for its current structure and results. This partnership has allowed us to integrate our backgrounds in improving the quality of work life for teachers, instructional design and improvement, program planning and evaluation, and teacher induction into the development of this research-based and dynamic structure for supporting new teachers. It is dynamic in that it develops the capacity of experienced educators to nurture new teachers in promoting improved student outcomes and, at the same time, enhances the school culture by promoting a culture of collaboration, research, and assessment of impact—the essential components of a Professional Learning Community.

Most important, we recognize that talented teacher leaders exemplify what Darling-Hammond (2003) calls "a valuable human resource for schools—one that needs to be treasured and supported" (p. 7). It is for them and for the bright, enthusiastic, and often intimidated teachers just entering the profession that we wanted to share what we have gained from our work in our own learning community. *Mentoring as Collaboration: Lessons From the Field for Classroom, School, and District Leaders* is filled with stories of those with whom we have worked who are exemplars in developing the confidence, competence, and skills of our next generation of teacher leaders.

Acknowledgments

This book is the outcome of many years of work and the contributions of talented and dedicated educators across our state. We designed a mentoring program for high-need schools nearly a decade ago. Since we first implemented it, we have expanded its focus to all school contexts and have incorporated numerous ideas shared by Mentor Core Teams across the state who have been implementing it in their schools. We have had the luxury of working with and learning from our colleagues at The University of Tennessee, Knox County Schools, and the Tennessee State Department of Education (TN SDE) as we have fine-tuned the program over the years. Lana Seivers, our state commissioner of education; Susan Bunch, the assistant commissioner for teaching and learning; Barry Olhausen, Executive Director, Office of Professional Development; and Elizabeth Vaughn-Neely, formally with TN SDE, have supported our work and facilitated its expansion statewide.

We especially want to thank our Knox County partners who have worked closely with us to expand the program districtwide. The Great Schools Partnership, led by a board of Trustees representing civic, business, district and higher education, and community leaders, has funded the expansion by providing professional development for new and expanding Mentor Core Teams. Donna Wright, the assistant superintendent, has supported the need to scaffold the induction of beginning teachers and has participated in helping us research and share data on program impact. Rodney Russell, the supervisor for professional development, has directed the districtwide expansion. He believes, as we do, that school-based Mentor Core Teams are the essential building block of effective mentoring and that the district must be capable of providing additional support where and when it is needed.

We have also worked very closely with a number of very talented teachers and principals who have taken our ideas, implemented them in their schools, shared what worked and what needed to be improved, and ultimately transformed their mentoring programs into communities of learning. They are the ones who encouraged us to write this book so that others could create similar school environments and legacies. Our special thanks to Sallee Reynolds and Greg Roach, principals of West High School in Knoxville, Tennessee, and to their committed faculty, for setting the "gold standard" for all of us. Their faculty led the program development along with numerous effective mentors over the past decade. Several graduates of The Urban Specialist Certificate Program have served Knox County Schools as teacher leaders in providing the professional development sessions for Mentor Core Teams. Beth Blevins, Julie Hembree, Mary Humphrey, Shannon Jackson, Theresa Nixon, Shannon Spirko, Bryan Paschal, Linda Smith, Anne Stinnett, and Vicki Wells, who first learned from us, have become our teachers as they have worked with our structure and training materials and suggested valuable refinements.

In addition, we thankfully acknowledge the support and assistance we received early in our careers by our mentors, Jerry and Elner Bellon. Our work with the Bellons on Shared Leadership and Improving the Quality of Work Life for educators was a catalyst for our systemic focus on induction. Our appreciation also goes to a number of university colleagues, especially Lynn Cagle, Susan Benner, and Bob Rider, who have supported our ongoing collaboration with public schools.

Most important, we want to thank our families and our husbands, Kermit and George, for their patience, encouragement, and support. They have made it possible for us to pursue our passion—promoting teacher quality and the environments in which they learn to teach.

PUBLISHER'S ACKNOWLEDGMENTS

Corwin Press gratefully thanks the following peer reviewers for their contributions to this book:

Dave F. Brown
Coauthor, *What Every Middle School Teacher Should Know*, Second Edition
Ardmore, PA

Janet Crews
Secondary Instructional Coach
Clayton School District
St. Charles, MO

Frank J. Masci
Professor, Department of Teacher Preparation
Johns Hopkins University
Baltimore, MD

Dennis Plyler, EdD
Little Rock, AR

About the Authors

Mary Ann Blank is wife of 38 years to husband, Kermit; mother to two wonderful, adult children, Kermit and Amy; and grandmother to tweens, Julia and Trevor. She is also a teacher educator who for many years has been a clinical professor at The University of Tennessee, Knoxville, working in professional development schools with preservice intern teachers. She also teaches courses on Instructional Design and Curriculum Planning and Development. With grant funding and assistance of other university and school system colleagues, she contributed to the development of a Teacher Leadership program for urban teacher leaders in a partnering school system and also to the Teacher Mentor Program shared with hundreds of educators across Tennessee. Mary Ann's long-standing concern for new teachers and for the school environments in which they learn to teach grew from her early encounters with "mentors" and anxieties about professional isolation. Through her dissertation on mentoring and review of the research ever since, she has attempted to use what she learned to help improve the quality of school life for all educators. She views *Mentoring as Collaboration* as another way to share what she now knows about the conditions needed to make the program work effectively and efficiently in schools and districts.

Cheryl A. Kershaw, married to husband, George, for 40 years, is the mother of two—Julie and Lindsay—and the grandmother of five—Alex, Andy, Jackson, Gavin, and Griffen. She began her career as an urban high school English teacher before becoming a clinical professor working with secondary preservice teachers in urban high schools and teaching courses in instruction, program design, and evaluation. For six years, she directed a Title II Teacher Quality Enhancement Grant, URBAN IMPACT, a partnership grant between The University of Tennessee, Knox County Schools, and the Tennessee State Department of Education. In this role she worked with university faculty and school district leaders in assuring that beginning teachers were better prepared to succeed in urban schools. This led to the development of The Urban Specialist Certificate Program, which tapped talented urban teachers, involved them in an intensive university/school system coursework, and provided teacher leadership roles for them in developing and refining mentoring programs. It was through this partnership and collaboration with university faculty, school and district leaders, and talented teachers that the mentoring program developed by the authors has grown from an innovative program for the schools with the highest teacher attrition rates into a districtwide approach to enhancing teacher quality. Since 2004 she has served as Executive Director of the Great Schools Partnership of Knox County Tennessee.

Part I

Mentoring

Putting the Research Into Practice

We share with many colleagues a strong concern for the quality of teachers and their teaching environments. Teacher effectiveness—what the teacher knows and can do in the classroom—is the most important factor in promoting student achievement. Research and common sense have long supported this notion. Teacher impact research (Cochran-Smith, 2003; Sanders, 2000) and analysis of teacher retention data and its correlation with student achievement (Darling-Hammond & Youngs, 2002) provide evidence that student achievement is clearly linked to teacher quality. Effective teachers manage to produce better achievement regardless of which curriculum materials, pedagogical approach, or reading program is selected (Allington, 2002).

We are also acutely aware of what Sparks (2002) describes as a decreased sense of "community, continuity, and coherence . . . driven not by too few teachers coming in, but by too many going out" (p. 1). In *Mentoring as Collaboration,* we recognize (but do not dwell on) the well-documented statistics about teacher retention and its correlation to teacher quality and student achievement. Instead, we are focusing on solutions—specifically, ways to attract and retain talented teachers, develop teacher leaders, and create energized learning communities where collaboration, assessment of impact, reflection, and improving outcomes for students create a motivating school culture for students and teachers. We are sharing our experiences and research-based strategies for "restoring hope" for those new teachers who enter the profession to make a positive difference in the lives of children (DuFour, DuFour, Eaker, & Karhanek, 2004). We have learned that a systemic focus on supporting new teachers and scaffolding their induction into the profession can reduce isolation within schools and systems and transform the ways educators work together to improve student outcomes. At a school level, this means that teacher leaders, along with their principal(s), develop action plans that are linked to their school's improvement plan to assure that new teachers are appropriately mentored in ways that directly impact their ability to make a difference with their students. At a system

1

level, central office personnel work with school administrators and teacher leaders to assure that they have the knowledge and resources to implement their mentoring program consistent with their improvement priorities. At the same time, system-level administrators hold high expectations for quality, monitor progress through systematic formative assessments, celebrate successes, and provide the vehicle for sharing across the district.

We address what Hord (2007) describes as "an important challenge for the next decade of teachers' professional learning . . . providing the opportunities—the structures and schedules—for school-based educators to come together to learn in community" (abstract). We agree that the current situation in many schools is one in which educators are physically isolated from colleagues by the "geography" of school facilities and the minute-to-minute schedules that all too often prevent ongoing dialogue and interaction. We also agree that collaborative learning results in more thoughtful decisions and solutions by allowing colleagues frequent opportunities to interact in studying their profession. But like others, we see that this type of collective learning is still not standard practice in many educational settings. The current and pervasive culture of isolation negatively impacts new teachers as they encounter these environments—and, it can no longer be tolerated. Nor can we continue to allow potentially talented new educators to sink before they have the chance to see that they can swim.

In *Mentoring as Collaboration,* we share a variety of "site-tested" structures and strategies that have been used to promote collaboration and a shared sense of responsibility for the success of new teachers. For the past ten years, we have promoted a *new way* of inducting teachers. We have been fortunate to gain inside knowledge from many diverse schools and districts that are "gearing up" to address the challenge of creating conditions that support collective learning in professional communities. We have learned from the "experts among us" (Schmoker, 2006) about the incredible commitment that can be generated when responsibility emanates from the "inside out." We have observed talented and committed individuals who contribute enthusiasm, energy, and the wisdom of experience to positively impact the entire organization as they accomplish the important work of mentoring. Our model was originally designed for high-need, high-turnover, and primarily urban schools. However, it has been successfully replicated in a wide variety of settings. We are sharing what we have learned from research and practice about the conditions, structures, and strategies needed to develop and sustain effective teacher mentoring programs; to build learning communities; to transform school cultures from isolated to interactive, sharing, and dynamic; and to promote the leadership of professionals at all career stages.

In *Mentoring as Collaboration,* we fully acknowledge the individual efforts of talented and committed mentors who work diligently with their new teachers to impart needed knowledge and skills to those who are just beginning their careers. Mentoring at the individual level is essential, and it is most often richly rewarding and empowering for both parties. As powerful as these individual relationships and interactions are, we have learned that they can be significantly enhanced through collective, focused efforts at the school and district levels. School-based actions magnify the individual efforts and greatly increase the level of professional learning throughout the organizations. Educators who are fortunate enough to work in schools with strong professional cultures understand and experience daily the benefits of collaboration and collegiality. They become fiercely committed to eliminating the isolation and lack of opportunities that can suppress the talents and enthusiasm of most new teachers. In a school-based structure for mentoring, we increasingly hear educators say *"it takes a 'village' to raise a novice."* That really says it all. They know that the "raising" must occur in schools with cultures that are supportive, positive, and professional. In these cultures, one of the norms becomes a high level of ownership for the critical task of mentoring. The task is distributed and the responsibility shared.

In addition, part of the ownership for new teacher support must also occur at the district level. School-based mentoring is most successful when a direct organizational link exists from the school to the district (and even beyond, to the state level). When the district culture also values professional learning and collaboration, the link can ensure the necessary support and coordination for mentoring and induction at the school and individual or classroom levels.

Guiding Principles for Effective Mentoring Programs

Our premise is that educators can (and must) provide a nurturing culture in every school and the needed assistance for new teachers in an organized, collegial, and efficient manner. Induction decisions require principals and teacher leaders to view student achievement as the standard that drives all decisions related to new teacher hiring, placement, and mentoring. Effective mentoring requires a well-planned program of experiences to ensure that all beginning teachers have opportunities to learn from their most talented colleagues, to be coached by highly effective mentors, and to be prepared to face the challenges that exist in every school context. We suggest the following principles, drawn from research and practice, to guide the development of your mentoring and induction program:

- *Our students can no longer afford "business as usual" in the induction of beginning teachers.* If we truly believe that teacher mentoring and student achievement are clearly linked, school administrators and leadership teams—in our case, the Mentor Core Teams—must recognize that their responsibility is to scaffold the transition from teacher preparation to in-service teaching. This means eliminating the historical "sink or swim" mentality; not giving new teachers the most difficult teaching assignments, particularly if they have had no experience with a subject or grade level; and not overburdening them with committee and extracurricular demands. It may even mean that hard decisions on staffing and facilities management must be made with the interests of student learning at the forefront of decision making.

- *Quality mentoring is the key, and induction assures it takes place.* While timeframes differ from one community or state to another, it is well recognized that teacher induction begins with preservice experiences and extends through the first several years of in-service teaching (often until tenure). It is dependent on high-quality mentoring, a well-organized structure, and a direct link to school leadership and school improvement efforts. An effective induction program has several critical components. First, it involves mentors who are talented teachers with the knowledge, skills, and dispositions to effectively nurture beginning teachers. This is a departure from the "rotation" or "it's my turn to have a student teacher" way of thinking—whether at the preservice or in-service stage. Mentors should have to *apply* for the role, and earning it should be formal recognition of the their capacity to serve as role models and coaches. Second, school-based programs, coordinated by a Mentor Core Team, should incorporate an intensive set of professional development experiences for both mentors and new teachers. These experiences should be designed to meet the needs and practical challenges that exist in the school and classrooms in which they are teaching. Third, these programs should be designed to assure effective mentoring in coaching new teachers to develop competencies aligned with INTASC (Interstate New Teacher Assessment and Support Consortium) standards that increase their ability to promote meaningful student learning. This often means differentiating the support for first-year teachers and for those with two or three years' experience by tailoring the support to the unique needs of each new teacher, regardless of years of experience.

> 66———— **A Comment From the Field** ————
>
> Even I was struggling with the challenges I would face in giving the new teacher my own classroom. My feeling was like that of my other experienced colleagues—I've been here 15 years and just got a classroom with a window! It is hard to imagine my having to "float" rather than making our new teacher do it. It was a difficult decision, but our entire department feels that it has paid off in terms of increased student achievement as well as satisfaction in "doing the right thing" for our new teachers.
>
> *Department Chair and Member of a Secondary Mentor Core Team*
> ————————————— 99

Finally, well-designed induction programs provide structured professional orientation tailored to each school's needs. They assure multiple levels of support extending beyond the typical assignment of a more experienced teacher to serve as a mentor to the novice teacher. Some schools are providing additional faculty support through "buddies" who coach in particular areas, retired teachers who serve on an "as needed" basis, new teacher advisors who serve as listeners and problem solvers, and "expert teams" in which all faculty members agree to share their areas of expertise on a variety of topics. Yet other programs, particularly in high-need schools with a history of teacher attrition and low student achievement, include specially trained, experienced external mentoring support personnel who can provide additional supervision, intensive coaching, modeling, "hands-on" assistance, and supplementary resources that go well beyond the time available to the school-based mentors. Often, external mentors are teachers released from the classroom for several years who return to the classroom after their term of service has concluded. In some school districts, usually those engaged in significant reform efforts, schools have specified a reduced teaching load (e.g., first few weeks of school, first semester, or first year) to provide time for the beginning teacher to observe other teachers; complete required professional development expectations; and consult with, plan, or coteach with an assigned mentor. Many include a tiered individualized professional growth plan that is developed to address the individual strengths and needs of each new teacher.

- *Effective induction offers beginning teachers the support they need in high-need schools.* High-need schools are, for the most part, those serving low-income, transient families, as well as students more at risk of failure. These students need the most effective and committed teachers in the profession to overcome the challenges and obstacles of poverty; parents with limited ability to assist in supporting student learning, families fearful of engaging with the school, and high mobility rates that continually place students in a series of "new" learning situations. All too often, these students enter high-need schools where there is also a continual revolving door of new teachers. What teachers and parents have known intuitively is that most new teachers are not as effective as most experienced teachers—and students learn less in their classes. This, according to Sanders and Horn (1998), becomes almost insurmountable if it occurs for three or more consecutive years. This situation continues to be especially important in high-need schools where students are frequently taught by one new teacher after another. The outcome is obvious: The children who need our best teachers are most often being taught by our beginning, least experienced teachers . . . year after year.

Johnson, Kardos, Kauffman, Liu, and Donaldson (2004) identified the differences between low-income and high-income schools in how mentoring occurs for new teachers. New teachers in low-income schools were less likely than their counterparts in high-income schools to benefit from mentoring and support by experienced colleagues; had fewer experienced mentors with expertise at the protégé's grade, subject, or even school level; and engaged in more sporadic conversations with their mentors that were frequently not related to issues of teaching and learning. Thus, beginning teachers in these high-need situations received neither substantive instructional support nor curricular guidance. Many ended up feeling unsuccessful as teachers and dissatisfied with their jobs.

Our recommendation for addressing these inequities is to establish a team of experienced teachers, the Mentor Core Team (MCT), to coordinate a structured program of broad, substantive support. MCTs, properly implemented, can promote professional learning that leads to increased teacher performance and student learning. Important conditions for high levels of impact are (a) clear roles and responsibilities, (b) clarity of purpose about the use of student data, (c) teachers' expertise and experience in identifying relevant research and best practices to increase student achievement (i.e., INTASC Standards), (d) active participation and carefully structured collaboration between teachers, and (e) opportunities for meaningful professional learning based on assessment data and related to key issues of everyday teaching and learning, which are sustained over time and of sufficient duration (Cohen & Hill, 1998; Desimone, Porter, & Garet, 2002; Feiman-Nemser, 2001; Garet, Porter, & Desimone, 2001; Kennedy, 1998; McLaughlin & Talbert, 1993).

> **" A Comment From the Field "**
>
> In our school system, we are finding that the Mentor Core Teams have influence beyond mentoring. They have become model Professional Learning Communities that serve as the "hub" for numerous support networks within the schools.
>
> *Assistant Superintendent for Instruction in a Large Metropolitan System*

- *Mentoring builds Professional Learning Communities (PLCs).* Research has shown, for some time, that traditional professional development, typically in the form of isolated training, does not improve teacher quality (Smylie, Allensworth, Greenberg, Harris, & Luppescu, 2001). However, when teachers learn to teach in a nurturing and supportive context, they are more focused on impacting student achievement than on merely surviving (Feiman-Nemser, 2001). Thus, mentoring is most powerful when it occurs within a context that is supportive and collaborative while holding high expectations for the performance of all—essentially a Professional Learning Community. We acknowledge that the solid foundation of induction programs is individual mentors, but we strongly feel that school-based support is equally, if not more, important. The development of novices in any organization is greatly influenced by the pervasive culture of the organization (Berliner, 1998). The ways individuals interact and relate to one another, the resources they have and how they are shared, the governance structures, and how decisions are made all impact the school culture and support systems. When schools and districts adhere to the principles of Professional Learning Communities, the widespread support and commitment to beginning teachers is transformed into practices that assure their access to the knowledge, skills, and experience of their colleagues. In this model, school-based support is provided in the form of a Mentor Core Team, which is viewed as one important professional learning team within the school that functions as PLCs should.

- *Mentoring and induction can accelerate new teachers' instructional effectiveness.* While educators have generally accepted the concept of mentoring as positive in socializing new teachers and contributing to the quality of their work lives, the "bottom line" indicator of impact is the academic growth of the students served. Ultimately, student achievement is the overarching goal of mentoring. Educators are beginning to realize that how a new teacher starts his or her career has a far greater impact on long-term teaching than does any preparation program. When novices experience quality induction during their first few years, they develop the knowledge, skills, and dispositions to teach successfully. It is important to note that a teacher's years of classroom experience do not necessarily translate to greater teacher quality, particularly after five years of experience (Mayer, Mullens, Moore, & Ralph, 2000; Rosenholtz, 1989; Wenglinsky, 2000). It is our belief and experience that how beginning teachers learn to teach in their first years influences their effectiveness throughout their careers. Thus, those who are mentored by knowledgeable, effective, nurturing role models will demonstrate those same behaviors as experienced teachers—and often earlier than their peers. When students respond positively to their instructional efforts, it is more likely that their confidence, work satisfaction, and sense of efficacy will commit them to a long life in the profession. Our research on impact has documented that effective mentoring has become a major strategy in accelerating the learning of effective teaching skills (Blank, Kershaw, Russell, and Wright, 2006).

> 66 ——— **A Comment From the Field** ———
>
> Everyone mentors new teachers in our school. Many have formal roles, but all will stop what they are doing to help a new teacher solve a problem or get what is needed. Many teach sessions for our monthly "Forums" or participate in coursework with interns. Over the past ten years, as our professional development school has matured, we have built a culture where we learn with and from each other. We even have our interns and new teachers team to provide professional development seminars—and find that this addresses a wider range of confidence levels with our more experienced faculty. New teachers are the ones who can really use technology to promote learning. So, we learn to control our machines from them and they learn to motivate and manage students from us! It's a win-win!
>
> *High School Professional Development School MCT Leader* 99

- *Mentoring transforms.* While the benefits of effective mentoring to beginning teachers have been clearly documented, it is less recognized that mentors benefit as well. Many cite rejuvenation, increased prestige accompanying the expanded role of teacher leadership beyond the classroom, opportunities to develop and share professional expertise, and the leaving of a legacy for their profession as among their most significant outcomes (Blank et al., 2006). Mentors are reinforced when their protégés become effective and efficient facilitators of learning incorporating research-based instructional, management, and assessment strategies. Studies show that, in the process of assisting others, mentors become more reflective of their own practices and consequently improve their own instructional effectiveness and sense of efficacy (Kershaw, Blank, Benner, Russell, Wright, Jackson, and Barclay-McLaughlin, 2006). We have found a high level of collaboration among mentors and their former protégés that has extended well beyond their formal mentoring relationship.

In addition, the benefits to the particular mentors and their new teachers, other educators in the school are transformed as well. When teacher turnover is reduced, the possibility of making progress on school improvement initiatives increases. Colleagues and administrators begin to see tangible progress and results. In addition, when the "right things" are happening in the classroom next door, everyone's job becomes easier and more satisfying. With lowered anxiety and frustration, a stronger sense of community, belonging, and collective ownership of results often develops. Mentoring is a way to increase professional sharing and to expand everyone's awareness of strengths and weaknesses in all grade levels and subject areas. The resulting professional culture increases shared responsibility for achieving priority outcomes.

ORGANIZATION AND USE OF THE BOOK

Mentoring as Collaboration: Lessons From the Field for Classroom, School, and District Leaders provides innovative ideas for building a school-based Teacher Mentoring Program that functions to promote professional learning throughout the school community. The book's purpose is to provide educational leaders with research-based information, structures, and specific strategies. Brief, ready-to-use/adapt resources are provided for tailoring the program to each school context. The organization of the book was designed to ensure direct attention to what the essential elements of a systemic, sustainable, and productive mentor program.

The organizing center is a brief survey, **Starting Point: Teacher Mentor Program Components Self-Assessment,** provided in the next chapter. It serves as a means for teachers and administrators to assess their current mentoring activities in relation to those recommended for a comprehensive teacher mentor program. We feel the survey has value in itself. It provides an opportunity to gather perceptions about the existing program (formal or informal) and focuses attention and discussion on the critical components of effective collaboration and teamwork for increasing student achievement. This is not a "top-down" program. Instead, it is meant to be transformative by engaging educators at all levels in identifying "what is" (the current status of mentoring) and tailoring "what ought to be" (mentoring that is systemic, collaborative, and research and data-based) to their own unique contexts. The remaining chapters provide "user-friendly" resources for administrators and teacher leaders to use or adapt when initiating a teacher mentor program or refining an existing one. The resources can be used in **Designing or Strengthening Your Mentoring Program (Part II), Implementing Your Teacher Mentoring Program (Part III), Assessing the Impact of Your Mentor Program (Part IV),** and **Growing and Sustaining Your Mentor Program (Part V).** Used in total or separately, the resources provide strategies to develop, implement, evaluate, and sustain programs that are clearly linked to the needs of new teachers, school contexts, and school improvement efforts.

In *Mentoring as Collaboration,* we do not propose that having a school-based mentor program is a "quick fix" for improving student outcomes. However, like all significant change efforts, it is part of the process and requires having a vision, resources, knowledge, skills, teamwork, and clearly defined plans and measurable outcomes. We believe that it is important to take a long-term view in building your teacher-mentoring program, but we are confident that you will see short-term impact by using the suggested structures and strategies. By choosing to implement the advocated strategies, you are investing in a process of promoting teacher leadership and generating shared responsibility for the success of new teachers and continuing to develop the school's most valuable resource—all teachers.

2

Getting Started

Teacher Mentor Program Components

Mentoring as Collaboration: Lessons From the Field for Classroom, School, and District Leaders is organized around the brief survey presented in this section. It identifies research-based components of productive mentor programs recommended by key researchers and refined by outstanding educators. It also prompts educators to determine if their current mentor program was designed effectively, is being implemented efficiently, and is producing the desired, positive impact. As is recommended in any organizational improvement effort, it is important to initiate the process of developing a new program or redesigning an existing one by assessing the current state of implementation. It is important to know "what is" before it is possible to clearly determine "what ought to be."

As we have shared our model throughout our state and with colleagues from many other states, it has become clear that mentoring is an appealing concept, but one that is open to varied interpretations and implementation approaches. We have found that most schools and school systems provide some degree of "in-house mentoring" for new teachers. The degree and type of mentor support vary greatly from school to school and system to system. In most, mentors are assigned to beginning teachers and work independently, and with mixed levels of success, in supporting their new colleagues. In some, mentoring is what we call a "hoped for" outcome. Mentors are assigned and, despite the best of intentions, do not have the time, knowledge, or skills to mentor effectively.

> **" A Comment From the Field**
>
> Before we realized what was involved in a real program, we had always assigned mentors to new teachers, but really didn't specify how their support should occur.
>
> We were very informal about the process— and, a lot was left to chance. We never were clear about what was expected or the responsibilities.
>
> *Middle School Principal* **"**

9

More formalized structures for mentoring tend to exist in schools and systems where leaders understand the link between mentoring and student achievement. Only a small percentage of schools or districts have a comprehensive, formalized program.

In our research, we have found that formalized school-based mentoring programs can provide a consistent, contextually relevant, and readily available support system tailored to the specific needs of new teachers. The most effective capitalize on opportunities, traditions, and special events to strengthen collaboration, collegial support, and learning-based interactions. As a result, they enhance the capacity to learn for all individuals (i.e., students, teachers, staff, administrators, parents, and community members) within the community and increase their feeling of satisfaction with schooling in general. The self-assessment provides baseline data regarding the *perceived* quality of a school or system mentoring program. The results, then, become the starting point for design or redesign.

RESEARCH-BASED COMPONENTS OF MENTOR AND INDUCTION PROGRAMS

Research, primarily from Ingersoll and Kralik (2004) and our own studies, is providing valuable information about components and conditions of effective mentor programs that lead to increased retention of new teachers. While research is continuing to uncover more about effective programs, the consensus is that few currently meet all the criteria identified below. Review of existing programs indicates that successful mentoring and induction programs should

- maintain a focus on student achievement and success;
- adhere to well-defined standards;
- provide assistance by mentors who are experienced teachers and well trained to be mentors;
- receive adequate funding;
- use a research-based evaluation process with their new teachers;
- extend beyond the first year of teaching experience with appropriate accommodations for teachers in their second and third years of teaching;
- function as part of a larger effort that provides additional support through reduced teaching loads, appropriate teaching assignment, ample opportunity for observation of other teachers, and targeted professional development;
- identify responsibility for program implementation and results;
- function as a collaborative partnership of district educators and higher education institutions responsible for teacher training;
- incorporate essential components, but be flexible enough to allow school (and district) educators to tailor strategies to fit specific contextual factors and to address the specific developmental needs of individual teachers;
- occur within a culture (state, district, school) that is supportive and encouraging professional development for both veterans and novices; and
- require, but differentiate, participation by novices depending on individualized needs and experiences.

STARTING POINT: A SELF-ASSESSMENT SURVEY

Use the survey to assess your current program. Review the results to identify strengths, gaps, redundancies, and/or differences in perceptions of implementation and/or effectiveness. We have seen the value of the survey in providing opportunities to gather perceptions on a broader scale about an existing program (formal or informal). It is appropriate for those at the beginning stages of designing a mentoring program, as it provides guidance in incorporating essential components. It is also appropriate for schools or systems with existing programs, as it affirms areas of strength that should be celebrated as well as areas in need of improvement.

The survey could be completed independently by individual educators or collectively by specific groups. If surveying individuals, it may be helpful to "code" (often by color) the survey so that it will then be possible to identify differences in perceptions. Suggested coding might include: (a) teachers with more than three years' experience, (b) teachers with fewer than three years' experience, (c) teachers who experienced their first two years in this school, (d) new mentors, (e) experienced mentors, and so on. The survey could also be completed collectively by grade-level or content-area teams.

✓ **Research to Practice Insight:** The self-assessment identified research-based components to incorporate in your school's or district's teacher mentor program. It is intended to "taken" and "discussed" by educators interested in creating a new program or redesigning an existing one. Guidelines are provided as to how to use the assessment, the results, and the resources provided. Even without the assessment, the resources in the remaining chapters are presented in "ready to use" form for educators engaged in strengthening and formalizing their teacher mentor programs.

STARTING POINT: TEACHER MENTOR PROGRAM COMPONENTS SELF-ASSESSMENT

	Our Current Teacher Mentor Program	*Strength of Our Program*	*Area to Strengthen*
Design or Redesign	1. Promotes a schoolwide understanding of and commitment to mentoring.		
	2. Is driven by clearly articulated and commonly understood goals.		
	3. Is coordinated by an active Mentor Core Team (MCT) composed of an administrator, a lead mentor, and qualified teacher mentors.		
	4. Has defined expectations, roles, and responsibilities for all MCT members.		
	5. Has defined criteria and procedures for mentor selection and assignments.		
	6. Ensures new teacher understanding of and commitment to mentoring expectations.		
	7. Is coordinated effectively to support new teachers.		
	8. Promotes meaningful professional learning and schoolwide collaboration.		
	9. Is allocated adequate time, resources, and support to perform mentoring responsibilities.		
	10. Includes operational guidelines and procedures to assure efficient meetings, effective problem solving, planning, and communication.		
Implementation	11. Facilitates appropriate professional development for mentors based on identified needs.		
	12. Uses new teacher needs assessment data to prioritize mentoring activities and develop individualized induction plans.		
	13. Provides appropriate mentoring activities to meet new teachers' social, emotional, and professional needs.		
	14. Assures mentors develop effective coaching strategies to promote new teachers' instructional effectiveness.		
	15. Uses evaluation data to improve program results (e.g., new teacher and mentor perceptions of support, school's professional climate for learning, instructional practices in classrooms, student achievement, teacher retention, and teacher leadership capacity).		
Assessment	16. Has a positive impact on school improvement priorities.		
	17. Is valued and supported by Central Office and linked to the system-wide improvement plan.		
	18. Contributes to individual and faculty-wide professional sharing and growth, teacher leadership, and capacity building.		
	19. Is structured to ensure continuous progress and sustainability.		
	20. Celebrates and recognizes the contributions of mentors and the accomplishments of beginning teachers.		

Copyright © 2009 by Corwin Press. All rights reserved. Reprinted from *Mentoring as Collaboration: Lessons From the Field for Classroom, School, and District Leaders* by Mary Ann Blank and Cheryl A. Kershaw. Thousand Oaks, CA: Corwin Press, www.corwinpress.com. Reproduction authorized only for the local school site or nonprofit organization that has purchased this book.

Guidelines for Using Survey Results

Survey results, item by item, could be shared and discussed to reach consensus on the program's current state. Table 2.1 below explains how each survey item indicates program design, implementation, impact, and sustainability. The discussion should be reinforcing when elements in the current program align with research recommendations. Another important by-product of the discussion is creative and collaborative thinking about how to incorporate specific structures and strategies that will strengthen every component of the current program.

● *Select and use How To steps and resources to initiate or strengthen your Mentor Program.* Beyond gathering perceptions and gaining focus, the major benefit of *Mentoring as Collaboration* is in providing resources related to each program component. Each of these components includes a brief rationale, with *How To* steps to achieve the desired outcomes. *Resources* are research-based and user-friendly. They present suggested professional development activities, forms, and checklists as well as insights from practitioners. The resources, selected based on feedback from colleagues about their usefulness and impact, are to be explored, used "as is," or adapted to meet the specific needs of the school. In other words, they are considered to be "best practice" for designing, implementing, evaluating, and sustaining a comprehensive teacher mentor program.

Table 2.1   Teacher Mentor Program

Teacher Mentor Program Survey Items	*Resources to Consider in Strengthening the Identified Program Components*
Program Design Items 1–9 focus on the basic elements of the overall program, emphasizing a comprehensive, sustainable, and team-based approach. Included are specific *How To* guidelines to assist the team in designing an effective program.	pages 15–53
Program Implementation Items 10–14 address professional development needs, teamwork processes, and coaching strategies. Included are specific *How To* steps for providing social-emotional support, orientation, and feedback for increased instructional effectiveness.	pages 60–103
Program Impact Items 15–20 focus on the impact of the program. Provided are *How To* strategies to assess a variety of new teacher, mentor, MCT, and student outcomes.	pages 104–139
Program Sustainability	pages 140–146

- *Think flexibly in making the Teacher Mentor Program model work in your school or system.* Each school (or district) has its own needs and strengths in supporting new teachers. Review the resources and select those structures and strategies that are the best match for your setting. Keep in mind that it is unlikely that any two programs will be exactly the same. Throughout *Mentoring as Collaboration* are samples from a range of schools and districts that are implementing the program in ways that fit their unique characteristics and needs. *How To* guidelines are provided, but flexibility in implementation is a key. In addition, we have included *Research to Practice Insights* that highlight exemplary practice.

- *Grow your program: Think BIG; Start Small.* The goal is to begin with a clear understanding of what it takes to build and sustain a productive mentoring program. Start with the end in mind—collaborating to strengthen the performance of beginning teachers, increasing the retention of capable new teachers, and improving outcomes for students. As you and your colleagues think creatively, brainstorm all the possible strategies. Then, get realistic in developing a long-range plan with timelines, responsibilities, and benchmarks. It is often advisable to implement the program in phases. Our caution is to avoid becoming so enthusiastic about all the possibilities that you try to do too much at once. Remember to initiate, develop, implement, assess, celebrate, and sustain what works—grow your program in stages and strengthen it over time.

66 —— **A Comment From the Field** ——

We were so excited about what we could do for our beginning teachers that we were wearing them and ourselves out! After the first semester, we decided that we were a bit overzealous—and exhausted. What we learned is that we need to set priorities and focus on the most important. It took awhile, but we now have the right balance.

Elementary Mentor Core Team

99

Part II

Designing or Strengthening Your Teacher Mentoring Program

Our proposal for quality teacher mentoring involves a comprehensive set of planned, purposeful activities with clear guidelines intended to ensure high-quality teaching and learning during a teacher's first years in the classroom. Within that definition are several key words—*comprehensive*, *planned*, *purposeful*, and *learning*. What we have seen in schools, even those where mentoring was considered well established, is random, sporadic activities that are primarily focused on socialization and on-the-spot problem solving. Though well intentioned, the majority lack structure and a formalized series of planned activities focused on promoting student learning. Few address the whole spectrum of new teacher needs, which range from providing social-emotional support and orientation to the new school culture to collaborating on planning, modeling best practices, and peer coaching. The research on effective mentoring underscores the importance of scaffolding beginning teachers' first years of teaching by mentors who are equipped to provide assistance as role models and coaches. It is at this level that mentoring has its greatest potential for improving student outcomes.

> **" A Comment From the Field "**
>
> Informal mentoring is a pervasive activity in schools, as most teachers are nurturers. Establishing a formal program in your school should not undermine the natural support system that exists informally. To fully induct novices so that they may be successful in today's world, it takes much more than relying on a few volunteer mentors.
>
> *Large School System's Supervisor of Professional Development*

Highly effective teacher mentoring programs involve significant planning and monitoring. In other words, it must be addressed as a *real* program with planning sessions, defined roles and responsibilities, resources, policies and procedures, scheduled activities, and accountability. A well-designed and implemented program not only supports new teachers but also builds and sustains multiple professional support systems in the school that contribute to a culture of collaboration and learning. A key to effective programs is a Mentor Core Team (MCT) that coordinates the program and assures that mentoring is recognized as essential to improving student achievement and increasing retention of quality novice teaches. Individual mentors are the teacher leaders who transform the "plan" into action as they support new teachers on an everyday basis.

The goal of Part 2 is to strengthen school-based teacher mentoring by moving from an informal, often sporadic approach to a formalized, systematic program—at the school and/or district level. If any items from 1 through 9 on the **Getting Started Self-Assessment** are areas to be strengthened, use the *How To* steps and tools below.

Designing or Strengthening Your Teacher Mentor Program

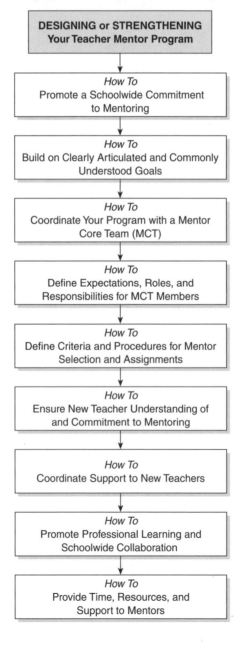

DESIGNING or STRENGTHENING
Your Teacher Mentor Program

How To
Promote a Schoolwide Commitment
to Mentoring

How To
Build on Clearly Articulated and Commonly
Understood Goals

How To
Coordinate Your Program with a Mentor
Core Team (MCT)

How To
Define Expectations, Roles, and
Responsibilities for MCT Members

How To
Define Criteria and Procedures for Mentor
Selection and Assignments

How To
Ensure New Teacher Understanding of
and Commitment to Mentoring

How To
Coordinate Support to New Teachers

How To
Promote Professional Learning and
Schoolwide Collaboration

How To
Provide Time, Resources, and
Support to Mentors

3

How to Promote a Schoolwide Commitment

The beliefs of educators who are developing, strengthening, or sustaining school-based mentoring help shape the action plans intended to support beginning teachers. Understanding faculty beliefs will help focus mentoring efforts, revise traditional practices, and build a sense of ownership for effective practices. Consistency and clarity about beliefs will make subsequent decisions and actions more straightforward and outcome-oriented.

Mentoring is a key strategy that must maintain high expectations for the learning of *all* students as its central focus. Experienced teachers are able to share their expertise with beginning teachers through a structured program that keeps improved student learning as the overarching goal.

Rather than assuming that all educators share similar beliefs regarding the importance of mentoring, it is helpful to initiate the goal-setting process with discussions of currently held beliefs and assumptions, found below in **Beliefs About Mentoring: A Survey**. As we all know from our own experiences, beliefs guide action. We want to ensure that all educators act in ways that are consistent with our common beliefs and understandings. If they understand that student achievement is hindered by high teacher turnover and the continual influx of new teachers, and believe that the way they approach teacher mentoring will make a difference, the outcome of the process will be improved student achievement, which is the bottom line for school improvement. Mentoring can help minimize the disruptive influences and be another major avenue for achieving the school's vision. The success cycle begins with progress on school improvement priorities and improved student achievement, and then continues with increased commitment to mentoring!

> 66 —— **A Comment From the Field** ——
>
> We had to change some attitudes about supporting new teachers—the "sink or swim" approach and the view that "I survived the trial by fire and so should they" had to go.
>
> *Elementary Principal*
>
> —— 99

17

BELIEFS ABOUT MENTORING: A SURVEY

Purpose: To review educator beliefs about mentoring, leading to a common understanding and consensus beliefs about mentoring

Timing: When initiating a program and yearly as a review

Indicate your perceptions of the following statements about mentoring. Responses will be tabulated and shared with the faculty as a beginning point of collegial discussion about values and strongly held beliefs that become the foundation of your program. Ultimately, accept, delete, or revise the statements to reflect your collective beliefs about mentoring.

	Strongly Disagree				*Strongly Agree*
1. Mentoring is one way to act on our expectation of maximum learning for *all* students.	1	2	3	4	5
2. Mentoring is one form of professional development all novice teachers should experience in the most positive ways.	1	2	3	4	5
3. Our mentors should be strong role models with outstanding experience and expertise to guide them in ways we value.	1	2	3	4	5
4. Mentoring should occur throughout every school day and be embedded in the work of teaching and learning— as is the case with all effective professional development.	1	2	3	4	5
5. Mentoring should capitalize on the unique strengths in our school (i.e., opportunities, programs, resources, and people).	1	2	3	4	5
6. Mentoring should occur in a school where the desire for improvement and lifelong learning is pervasive.	1	2	3	4	5
7. Mentoring is integral to school improvement efforts and a way for us to progress on our priorities.	1	2	3	4	5
8. Mentoring should be an important way for teachers to develop their leadership abilities.	1	2	3	4	5
9. Mentoring occurs best in a school where all educators willingly support and contribute to the development of novice teachers.	1	2	3	4	5
10. Mentoring significantly contributes to novices' opportunities to learn to teach. However, in our school we need to provide other accommodations to support our new teachers.	1	2	3	4	5

Copyright © 2009 by Corwin Press. All rights reserved. Reprinted from *Mentoring as Collaboration: Lessons From the Field for Classroom, School, and District Leaders* by Mary Ann Blank and Cheryl A. Kershaw. Thousand Oaks, CA: Corwin Press, www.corwinpress.com. Reproduction authorized only for the local school site or nonprofit organization that has purchased this book.

Discussion Starters:

☛ Which beliefs do a majority of our faculty currently relate to strongly?

☛ Which need more discussion to gain consensus?

☛ Which are not needed, inappropriate, or hold no meaning for us?

4

How to Build on Common Goals

Another significant step in formalizing your mentor program is to attend to the sometimes tedious task of identifying clear goals, specific outcomes, and action plans. While the most obvious goal of mentoring is to retain new teachers, perhaps the more significant desired outcomes are to maximize student learning, to increase positive attitudes toward learning, and to transform schools into real communities of professional learning. We have found that effective

mentoring has helped our beginning teachers be able to perform more like their experienced colleagues—and, in less time than their peers who lack the strong guidance provided by an effective teacher serving as a mentor. Therefore, the focus of your mentor program should be threefold— your beginning teachers, the students they teach, and the mentoring faculty.

The following examples illustrate why and how two very different schools established the goals for their mentor programs. We feel they both highlight the need to have these conversations!

> **66 ——— A Comment From the Field ———**
>
> Our goals for mentoring are fairly simple: to increase student achievement and student motivation to learn. We do this by helping our novices be effective everyday as they teach. We want to retain capable new teachers by increasing their satisfaction with teaching in our school.
>
> *High School Administrator* **99**

CONSENSUS BELIEFS TO GOALS FOR THE TEACHER MENTOR PROGRAM: TWO EXAMPLES

Purpose: To ensure clear articulation and understanding of program goals

Timing: When initiating a program and yearly as a review

Example 1: Goals for a High-Need Middle School Teacher Mentor Program

Context: This high-need middle school has long engaged in ongoing but informal efforts to stop the exodus of eager but inadequately prepared novice teachers who found themselves assigned to a teaching position with which they had little familiarity. After learning about the successes of another elementary school with a well-established mentor program, the faculty decided to create their own program. Their starting point was a collegial discussion about their desires for the program.

Goals and Objectives: Most faculty recognized the need to do some things differently related to their beginning teachers. With this awareness established, the faculty was then able to formulate their need to attract and retain talented teachers in the following goals:

#1. Reduce teacher turnover. The faculty freely shared their frustration at constantly "training" new teachers only to have them transfer to other schools with possibly less-challenging students. In addition, they realized the limits of their energy and ability to meet the wide-ranging needs of their novice teachers. Retaining promising teachers was to be the major focus of their program for several years.

#2. Increase novice teacher commitment to urban education. The faculty and administration also shared their desire to find potential teachers who are the "best fit" for their students. Several faculty members who had been mentors were well aware of the school system's traditional hiring practice of "requiring" new teachers to "pay their dues" in this school before being allowed to transfer to another school. The team decided to involve mentors more actively in the interview process to attempt to identify the most likely prospects to hire—those with a strong desire to teach in their setting and an optimistic but realistic outlook about the potential challenges. (As a side note, after this process had been in place for several years, one added benefit of having mentors involved in the interviews was their increased commitment to active mentoring and visible support for school improvement efforts.)

66 —————— **Comments From the Field** ——————

We have always mentored, but there was not widespread ownership. To establish a real program, we knew that we needed to confront some long-standing and wrong-thinking beliefs about "paying your dues" and "entitlement." In the process of sharing our expectations and coming to a common understanding about mentoring, we "uncovered" some beliefs that were counter to our direct focus on teacher performance and its important link to student achievement and positive student attitudes toward learning. We are now using our mentor program as another way to communicate, model, foster, and monitor the consistency of our expectations with our actions.

Middle School Administrator

Teacher mentoring *must* be seen as a priority in our school—and our system. Retaining capable new teachers and growing them into effective, caring teachers and supportive colleagues ARE important ways to increase student achievement and meet our improvement goals. It is all about the kids!

Veteran Elementary Teacher

99

Example 2: Goals for a High-Performing High School in a Large Metropolitan City

Context: This comprehensive high school had a well-established and valued mentor program. The leadership team attributed the current strength of the program to the active support of the administration. However, the school was soon to experience a change in its leadership. The faculty who served as mentors wanted to develop a strategy that would ensure the continued support of the "new" administrator. One important activity was to create written documentation defining mentoring goals, expectations, activities, and outcomes.

Program Goals: Input was elicited from most of the faculty members, including current and former novice teachers. The result of this activity was the generation of several important reasons for continued quality mentoring. This information was then consolidated into consensus statements and presented as goals of the school's mentor program.

#1. Increase student academic performance and motivation to learn. To sustain the school's strong academic reputation and its strength in meeting the needs of all levels of learners, there were strong feelings among faculty about the desire to have their reputation continue. With the annual entry of new teachers, the faculty had seen how important it is to "grow" them into the kind of caring and effective teachers they were replacing. They had seen that with the support and assistance of mentors, most novice teachers had clearly demonstrated their ability to connect with their students, improved their instructional effectiveness, and developed a stronger sense of efficacy.

#2. Increase levels of satisfaction with the profession. Most current faculty showed true enjoyment with being teachers in this school. A frequently expressed statement is, "I love coming to work every day." The feeling was that if novices received the needed assistance to successfully negotiate the numerous perils experienced by many beginning teachers, they would feel high levels of satisfaction with their current teaching assignment and a sense of belonging and commitment. Simply, if novices received support, were able to develop personal and professional relationships, and were successful with the students, they would stay at the school and feel highly satisfied with their choice to teach.

> 66 ——— **A Comment From the Field** ———
>
> I needed mentoring when I had a student who was visually impaired in my class. Everyone assumed that I knew how to accommodate to meet this student's needs, but, even as an experienced teacher, I didn't! At times, every teacher needs access to mentoring assistance.
>
> *High School Science Department Head*
> 99

#3. Increase sharing in a school culture that values professional learning. The faculty believed that mentoring is a powerful way to transmit professional knowledge and skills, as well as to instill an enthusiasm for lifelong learning. Moreover, the mentor program had significantly contributed to their development of an intellectually stimulating professional culture by capitalizing on everyone's strengths and expanding overall awareness of school expectations and shared responsibility for achieving priority outcomes. Mentors and other veterans in this school have benefited from a supportive culture where professional sharing is highly valued.

5

How to Coordinate Your Program With a Mentor Core Team (MCT)

The school's Mentor Core Team (MCT) is the leadership team established to ensure the quality of mentoring support experienced by new teachers. The MCT monitors the support to promote some uniformity, while also providing flexibility and individualization, in experiences and expectations so that the specific needs of beginning teachers are met.

Many educators have found that high-quality teacher mentoring takes more than sporadic leadership. School-based teams are needed to move mentoring from randomly successful to well-structured, systemic plans that are integral to the way they work together to improve student achievement. Researchers have documented the importance of having teams of teachers working together to improve student achievement (Roberts & Pruitt, 2003; Schmoker, 2001). In applying this to the support of beginning teachers, Johnson and colleagues (2004) studied the differences in how mentoring occurs for new teachers in low-income schools and for those in high-income schools (Johnson et al., 2004). One of their main findings was that a support gap exists: New teachers in low-income schools are less likely than their counterparts in high-income schools to benefit from mentoring and support by experienced colleagues. The low-income schools had fewer experienced mentors with expertise related to their new teachers' grade, subject, or school needs. The discussions between mentors and their protégés were characterized as sporadic

66 —— **A Comment From the Field** ——

We found that establishing a leadership team was our most important step in formalizing our mentor program. Prior to that we had many well-intentioned efforts, but no means to link our mentoring to our ongoing school improvement efforts. The MCT provided us with the link!

Lead Mentor

99

and not about issues of teaching and learning, which meant that novices received neither substantive instructional support nor curricular guidance. Sadly, the outcomes for most novices were limited success with students and dissatisfaction with their professional roles. The researchers' recommendation for addressing these patterns of differences and inequity was to establish a team of experienced teachers to serve as mentors to provide broad, substantive support (see the guidelines below for information on how to establish an MCT). Their research is consistent with our own findings (Blank et al., 2004) that teacher induction, when planned and implemented by high-functioning teams, is more effective and purposeful in both identifying and addressing the needs of beginning teachers. When implemented by low performing MCTs, the mentoring program emphasis was directed more toward socialization and on-the-spot problem solving. The higher performing teams directed their efforts more toward enabling the beginning teacher to improve teaching and learning through collaboration and planning, peer coaching, and involving the novice in appropriate professional development activities. Those most focused on professional development recognized that they had overlooked some important needs for socialization that should be included in their program refinement.

CREATING AN MCT: GUIDELINES

Purpose: To establish an ongoing (or permanent) school-level leadership team that is responsible for "quality assurance" in designing, implementing, assessing, and adjusting mentoring experiences

Timing: When designing the program

Several important decisions should be made in creating an effective leadership team and in determining how it will function within the school context. The size of the team should be large enough to assure that beginning teachers at any grade level or in any subject area have someone who has assumed responsibility for making their transition to teaching successful. Keep the size manageable—over 10 is too large! Consider the following questions, suggestions, and examples (see Table 5.1) in designing the structure of your Mentor Core Team:

> **66** ———————————— **Comments From the Field** ————————————
>
> Our MCT members essentially assume responsibility for socializing beginning teachers into their new school environment, providing assistance necessary to meet the many challenges of the profession, and working closely with a designated administrator and colleagues to ensure high-quality learning experiences. Our MCT has also been essential in promoting schoolwide collaboration.
>
> *High School Mentor*
>
> Many of my administrator colleagues are finding that a major obstacle to sustaining school improvement is the transience of faculty members. With new teachers coming in, we have to be sure that they attend to our priorities with the strategies we identified. We have come to realize that mentoring must be a well-designed, systematic approach.
>
> *Elementary Principal*
>
> **99**

> ❝—————————————— **Comments From the Field** ——————————————
>
> When we became aware of the team approach to mentoring, we felt that structure would help us meet our needs in mentoring new teachers. We had not yet stabilized our faculty to the point where we had enough potential mentors with classroom experience or proven skill to be mentors.
>
> *Middle School Member of MCT*
>
> What we are seeing currently is that more of the assistance new teachers need to learn to teach effectively is left to the schools. It is critical that the state and district provide additional support. When you have a couple of alternatively certified teachers who are learning everything about teaching in your school, it falls to you and your colleagues to do what needs to be done.
>
> *Assistant Principal at a Large High School*
>
> We have found that having a talented, trained Mentor Core Team has had numerous benefits for our school. First, these teachers have had special training on effective instruction that goes beyond our traditional staff development. Second, what they are providing to beginning teachers through their one-on-one coaching and "forums" is exceptional. More important, though, they're beginning to entice their more experienced colleagues into participating—and learning. Not everyone on our staff—or even on the Mentor Core Team— is actually mentoring. They are, however, contributing to mentoring in some capacity. Some lead seminars, others teach special classes for our interns, and others lead informal lunch or after-school problem solving sessions. We also have created "expert teams" for all faculty to share their expertise—organized, updated, and scheduled by our MCT coordinator.
>
> *High School Principal*
>
> In our school, the paraprofessionals play an important role in providing some literacy support and tutoring. Although the assistants are all "highly qualified," they were not prepared to provide instructional services without some professional development.
>
> Our MCT decided that one of the best ways to help the assistants be effective in their roles was to assign each a mentor to provide support through modeling, observation, and feedback.
>
> *Elementary Principal*
>
> ————————————————————————————————————❞

Table 5.1   Guidelines for Creating a MCT

Who should be members of the MCT?	Suggestion: School administration and teacher leaders
	• A building-level administrator ("Required!")
	• An appropriate number of teacher leaders, representative of grade or school levels (elementary/middle school) or departments (secondary) and a representative from special instructional areas
	• Most MCTs include one Special Educator.
	• Some MCTs involve a parent or community leader (optional).

Who selects members of the MCT?		**Suggestion: Link the selection process to school leadership** • The school leadership team • Some schools nominate members. • One member of the MCT should be represented on the school's leadership team.
What qualities should MCT members possess?		**Suggestion: Involve highly effective teachers who** • are positive professional role models; • are respected teacher leaders; • have experience in the school (preferably at least two years); • have awareness of new teacher needs and concerns; • demonstrate a commitment to their own professional growth and that of their colleagues; • are willing to be or are trained as a mentor; • are capable of facilitating professional development for colleagues; and • are willing to assume school-based teacher leadership roles that may involve additional time and effort beyond their own teaching responsibilities.

How many teacher members should be on the MCT?		**Suggestion: The size of the MCT depends on the context of the school. In addition to an administrator, each MCT should be comprised of a combination of mentoring teachers who represent the needs of the new and experienced faculty requiring their services.**
		• High-turnover schools need a representative from each grade level, content area, or department and someone to represent special areas
		    o *Elementary School Example:* the administrator, one teacher per grade level, and another teacher representing special areas
		    o *Middle or High School Example:* an administrator, one person per core content area, and (at least) one special areas teacher
		• Low-turnover schools (one or two new teachers per year) need far smaller MCTs
		    o *Elementary School Example:* one teacher for primary grades and another for intermediate grades.
		• Additional "voices" can be added to teams as needed: teachers new in their careers (two to three years of experience), parents or community members (for home-school or community support)

Table 5.1   (Continued)

What qualities should the Lead Mentor, the coordinator of the MCT, possess?		**Suggestion: Every MCT needs a leader who takes responsibility for overseeing and coordinating the varied roles and responsibilities. The educator who serves as the coordinator should** • exhibit organizational and management skills; • be knowledgeable about research of "best practices" in instruction and assessment; • demonstrate proven or potential leadership skills; • be committed to mentoring; • be willing to devote the time and energy to make mentoring experiences positive for everyone involved.
Who is to be served by the Mentor Program?		**Suggestion: To avoid possible problems or misunderstandings later, it is important to specify who will receive mentoring. Decisions about who is to be served may relate to available resources (especially if compensation is involved). Teachers in all the following categories need mentor support and assistance to some extent. Be sure to keep an open "invitation" allowing any teacher to choose to be mentored.** • First-year teachers • Second- and possibly third-year teachers who are not yet tenured • Teachers who are new to the school, system, or state • Teachers who are assigned a grade level or content area with which they lack experience • Long-term substitute teachers who are filling in on an extended basis • Preservice teachers (field experience, student teachers, or interns) • Experienced teachers who need and/or seek support or assistance

✔ **Research to Practice Insight:** Research is showing the benefits of mentoring beyond the first year. We have found that when novices are mentored by conscientious mentors who are also highly effective teachers, the instructional effectiveness learning curve of the novices can be greatly accelerated. Thoughtful decisions need to be made about how to mentor second and even third year teachers in ways that address their needs—not replicating what they have already experienced as first year teachers.   —The Authors

6

How to Define Roles for MCT Members

Mentor Core Team members are the "front line" in overseeing all mentoring activities. They design, implement, and coordinate all mentoring activities and study the impact of their efforts to assure a seamless transition for teachers from preservice to in-service teaching. This includes designing and facilitating mentoring activities, selecting mentors and pairing them with protégés, and ensuring that the needs of beginning teachers are addressed. Most teams contribute to or actually lead educators in their schools in designing job-embedded professional development opportunities for both beginning and experienced teachers. Like all teams, the MCT will function most effectively and efficiently with clarity about their roles and responsibilities.

The most effective Mentor Core Teams are led by a Lead Mentor, for whom this is a schoolwide leadership role. The Lead Mentor coordinates the work of the team with the school administrator and the school leadership team to assure that mentoring is a central focus of school operations and improvement efforts and to assure program continuity and sustainability. The Lead Mentor role involves a number of formal and informal responsibilities that take time, interpersonal skills, and organizational talent. The Lead Mentor should be included on the school's leadership

> 66 —————— **A Comment From the Field** ——————
>
> The quality of our Mentor Program is attributed to the strength and energy of our MCT. The inclusion of our administrator on the MCT has also made a huge difference in the quality of support we now provide. We know that the administrator's involvement sends the message to the faculty that mentoring is a priority. But, perhaps the more important reason is that all too often decisions about new teacher assignments and responsibilities are already made before mentoring ever begins. Allowing the administrator opportunities to collaborate with MCT members can greatly influence the parameters of teaching assignments before situations become those that set novices up for failure.
>
> *Former New Teacher and*
> *Member of the School's MCT*
> 99

team to align mentoring with all other school operations and initiatives. The leadership position could be rotated periodically or assigned as a long-term teacher leadership role. As with all productive teams, leadership is key.

The importance of administrator involvement and support is critical to realizing intended results from your Mentor Program. A building-level administrator is a "required" member of the MCT. Experience has shown that decisions about how new teachers are inducted into the profession need to be made collaboratively (by teacher leaders AND an administrator). Many benefits can be realized because of the administrator's regular attendance at MCT meetings and activities. Their input is critical on key decisions related to new teachers' conditions for learning to teach. Because of their involvement, administrators develop a heightened understanding of the perils of allowing novices to accept or be assigned overly challenging assignments.

Review the following suggested duties for the key participants of your mentor program. Edit the listings to identify the duties determined to be relevant and appropriate responsibilities for your school setting and situation. We leave the specific decisions to educators who best know the context to ensure alignment with the unique characteristics of each school setting.

66 ——— **A Comment From the Field** ———

I believe that the principal's involvement shows visible and intentional commitment to productive mentoring. Principals demonstrate their commitment by attending MCT meetings when possible or reviewing meeting summaries to stay current on events when attendance is not possible. They should also respond to questions raised by the team, take recommended actions, and/or provide necessary resources. Therefore, overt support from building-level administration is critical to making any school-based mentor program successful.

Lead Mentor

99

EXPECTATIONS AND RESPONSIBILITIES FOR MCT MEMBERS: CHECKLIST

Purpose: To clearly communicate mentor team member roles

Timing: When designing the mentor program

Review these suggested duties for Mentor Core Team members. Identify the ones that would be appropriate responsibilities for your team members. Add or delete as is relevant for your school setting. Collectively, the purpose of the duties is to strengthen leadership, organization, and coordination.

_____ Serve as advocates for mentoring and for all beginning teachers. This ranges from introducing new teachers to the faculty to assuring that difficult organizational decisions are based on student needs, not seniority.

_____ Oversee all mentor activities for beginning teachers.

_____ Select, assign (or pair), and support mentor(s).

_____ Coordinate all support provided to beginning teachers, including that from the assigned mentor(s) and from any additional school-level and external support providers.

_____ Conduct systematic assessments of program implementation and impact and use data for decisions about program refinements. (See Part IV for sample assessments and data collection forms.)

_____ Identify necessary record-keeping activities and accountability procedures for mentors.

_____ Identify accountability procedures for new teachers. Determine necessary documentation related to required teacher evaluation process or to individualized induction plans.

_____ Collaborate with administrators and colleagues to ensure widespread ownership of the mentor program.

_____ Function as a high-performing team and model a Professional Learning Community.

Copyright © 2009 by Corwin Press. All rights reserved. Reprinted from *Mentoring as Collaboration: Lessons From the Field for Classroom, School, and District Leaders* by Mary Ann Blank and Cheryl A. Kershaw. Thousand Oaks, CA: Corwin Press, www.corwinpress.com. Reproduction authorized only for the local school site or nonprofit organization that has purchased this book.

EXPECTATIONS AND RESPONSIBILITIES FOR THE LEAD MENTOR: CHECKLIST

Purpose: To clearly communicate expectations

Timing: When designing the mentor program

Review these suggested duties for the Lead Mentor. Identify the ones that would be appropriate responsibilities for your mentor coordinator. Add or delete as is relevant for your school setting. Collectively, the duties should identify relevant and clear expectations.

_____ Work collaboratively with others in determining policies and procedures for the mentoring program.

_____ Promote productive mentoring by facilitating constructive problem solving related to mentoring challenges and possible conflicts.

_____ Collaborate with MCT members to organize and facilitate professional development activities for beginning teachers.

_____ Collaborate with MCT members to assign mentors to beginning teachers.

_____ Determine professional development needs of mentors.

_____ Determine professional development needs of new teachers.

_____ Organize MCT meetings and maintain records of mentoring activities.

_____ Collaborate with MCT members to implement formative and summative evaluations and to use the data to improve the mentor program.

_____ Maintain regular contact and open communication with administrator, mentors, and new teachers.

_____ Confer with the MCT members regarding *need to know* information and decisions related to the mentoring.

_____ Work with others to identify ways to celebrate progress and successful completion of the first year (including ways to show appreciation and public recognition).

Copyright © 2009 by Corwin Press. All rights reserved. Reprinted from *Mentoring as Collaboration:Lessons From the Field for Classroom, School, and District Leaders* by Mary Ann Blank and Cheryl A. Kershaw. Thousand Oaks, CA: Corwin Press, www.corwinpress.com. Reproduction authorized only for the local school site or nonprofit organization that has purchased this book.

EXPECTATIONS AND RESPONSIBILITIES FOR THE ADMINISTRATOR: CHECKLIST

Purpose: To clearly communicate expectations

Timing: When designing the mentor program

Review these suggested duties for the school administrator. Identify the ones that would be appropriate responsibilities. Add or delete as is relevant for your school setting. Collectively, the purpose of the duties is to identify relevant and clear expectations.

_____ Hire the very best qualified candidates (involving MCT members in the hiring process).

_____ Avoid overly taxing teaching and extracurricular assignments for new teachers.

_____ Maintain a safe, secure, intellectually stimulating, professional, and collaborative school environment.

_____ Promote productive mentoring throughout the school.

_____ Welcome and orient new teachers to the school.

_____ Collaborate with MCT members to secure necessary teaching resources for new teachers.

_____ Have frequent contact with new teachers to build positive relationships.

_____ Resolve any problems beyond the scope or authority of the Lead Mentor and MCT members.

_____ Provide needed resources for mentoring activities.

Copyright © 2009 by Corwin Press. All rights reserved. Reprinted from *Mentoring as Collaboration: Lessons From the Field for Classroom, School, and District Leaders* by Mary Ann Blank and Cheryl A. Kershaw. Thousand Oaks, CA: Corwin Press, www.corwinpress.com. Reproduction authorized only for the local school site or nonprofit organization that has purchased this book.

7

How to Select Mentors and Assignments

I t is critical to select the "right" educators to be mentors. It has been our experience that not all educators, even those performing at high levels, possess the expertise, experience, skills, and dispositions to be effective mentors. In most schools, the selection and assignment of mentors are established practices, but are generally "unofficial" or informal and usually not strategic. While many educators who have served as mentors have had significant and positive impacts on their protégés, others have not. Wong (2001) reported that 25 percent of beginning teachers continue to rate the mentoring they received as poor. One of the significant reasons for this perception was that no systematic procedures were in place to ensure that careful, professional thought was applied when choosing mentors and matching them with protégés. Often, mentor selection and pairing decisions are made solely by principals, eliminating the potential of more appropriate pairings that result from collaboration with teacher leaders. Our major goal, regardless of the numbers of novices to be served, is that each new teacher be assigned an appropriate mentor committed and capable of providing quality support (see **Pairing Mentors with Beginning Teachers: Guidelines**).

> ❝ ────── **A Comment From the Field** ──────
>
> It is no longer the sole decision of the principal as to who should mentor, and it is certainly not decided on the basis of some rotation (or "your turn") system. We try to ensure every new teacher has access to a quality mentor who is also an effective teacher.
>
> *Assistant Principal in a Middle School* ❞

Another probable cause of the poor mentoring rating is that in many cases mentors were selected and assignments made with little or no accountability or follow-through. Other negative factors cited most frequently are unclear expectations (see **Expectations and Responsibilities for Mentors: Checklist**), lack of opportunity to interact (usually due to lack of proximity), limited time, mentoring assignments viewed as an "add-on" responsibility, inadequate preparation to be mentors, and inadequate on-site or district support (Wong, 2001). Selecting the "right" mentors and matching them strategically is the result of thoughtful and purposeful decisions (see the following guidelines for mentor selection criteria, selection process, and application form).

SELECTION CRITERIA: GUIDELINES

While it may seem intuitive, identifying specific characteristics will lead to productive selection criteria for mentors. The essential question for accomplishing this task is

Which characteristics of mentors are especially important to us?

- *willingness and eagerness to be a mentor* (being allowed to opt out if personal and other professional responsibilities are "too much" at the time)
- *competence as an instructor* (in addition to content knowledge, has expertise in critical instructional areas such as planning, management, teaching strategies, and assessment)
- *experience at the school site* (knows the school's culture, context, community, rituals, and, perhaps most important, its "unwritten" rules)
- *people and help orientation* (values diversity, enjoys working with people, and is naturally nurturing)
- *active listening skills* (is perceptive, sensitive, and empathetic)
- *competence as a communicator* (can give feedback and advice constructively and clearly)
- *open-mindedness* (can analyze situations from varying perspectives and is nonjudgmental)
- *sound professional judgment* (helps novice avoid problems and shows common sense)
- *resourcefulness* (exhibits a "can-do" approach and optimism)
- *political astuteness* (knows the informal power structure and can use it effectively)
- *sense of humor* (often gets us through the day)

SELECTION PROCESS: GUIDELINES

Suggestions:

- The MCT has the responsibility for selecting mentors.
- Being selected as a mentor is an "earned" honor.
- "Mentors-in-Training" can participate in a variety of ways to support their new colleagues—as "buddies" who check in frequently, as experts sharing some "best practice," as models demonstrating some specific teaching strategy or routine, and so on.
- Use a formalized application process for selecting mentors or employ a nomination process, either self-nominated or recommended by a colleague. The intent is to elevate the professional status of being a mentor.
- Do not have an "open call" for mentors or a faculty "vote" on who should be mentors.
- Increase the numbers of new teachers who are the beneficiaries of effective mentoring—they then aspire to become mentors.

MENTOR APPLICATION: SAMPLE FORM

Purpose: For the Lead Mentor and MCT to use in identifying potential mentors and areas of faculty expertise, interest, availability, schedule, and so on in working with new teachers

Timing: Prior to or at the beginning of the year (spring would be ideal)

Our Mentor Core Team has developed several important beliefs about mentoring that guide our efforts to select the *right* educators to serve as primary mentors to our new teachers. We believe that

- mentoring is a way of assuring that our students have teachers who have the knowledge, skills, and attitudes to work effectively with students of diverse abilities and interests;
- new teachers need exemplary role models committed to working with them;
- new teachers need to experience all aspects of the school environment and school community; and
- effective mentors are competent professionals who are people- and help-oriented, empathetic listeners, open-minded, resourceful, and willing to coach beginning teachers in various aspects of their professional growth.

We encourage you to become a mentor if you are willing to serve in any of the following capacities: mentor, coach, facilitator, role model, instructor, liaison, and/or advocate to our new teachers. Please complete the attached form to let us know the roles you are willing to assume.

— —

Name _____

_____ Mentor (Primary or Secondary)

_____ Expert (content or pedagogy)

_____ Model (for observations)

_____ Instructor for preservice teacher coursework

_____ Facilitator of community mapping

_____ Facilitator of service learning

_____ Facilitator of action research

_____ Facilitator of "brown bag chats"

_____ Instructor on the teacher evaluation process

_____ Advisory board member

_____ Buddy

_____ Other (Please describe)

**Please feel free to add any other information that will help us plan for next year.
Thank You!**

Copyright © 2009 by Corwin Press. All rights reserved. Reprinted from *Mentoring as Collaboration: Lessons From the Field for Classroom, School, and District Leaders* by Mary Ann Blank and Cheryl A. Kershaw. Thousand Oaks, CA: Corwin Press, www.corwinpress.com. Reproduction authorized only for the local school site or nonprofit organization that has purchased this book.

EXPECTATIONS AND RESPONSIBILITIES FOR MENTORS: CHECKLIST

Purpose: To clearly communicate expectations

Timing: When implementing the mentoring program

Review these suggested duties for mentors. Identify the ones that would be appropriate for your school setting or revise. Collectively, the purpose is to identify relevant and clear expectations.

_____ Develop an understanding of your teacher leadership role as mentor.

_____ Develop an understanding of your responsibilities as a member of the mentoring team.

_____ Collaborate with our Lead Mentor to productively resolve any mentor-related challenges.

_____ Work with the MCT to orient your protégé to the important internal and external expectations of teachers as professionals.

_____ Work with the MCT to acquire the necessary resources, materials, equipment, and supplies for your protégé.

_____ Work with the MCT to orient your protégé to the important resources, necessary information, and important contacts in your school, community, and district.

_____ Complete the required paperwork and accountability forms.

_____ Model your ability to balance your own work and life responsibilities with your responsibilities for mentoring.

_____ Become knowledgeable about the teacher evaluation process your protégé will experience.

_____ Provide input in developing your protégé's Induction Plan and guidance in achieving it.

_____ Model "best practices" and research-based teaching strategies for effective planning, teaching, classroom management, and assessment.

_____ Conduct observations of your protégé—share information in a way that recognizes progress and guides reflection and problem solving.

_____ Model your disposition of lifelong learning and contribute to the professional growth of your colleagues as well as your protégé.

_____ Provide suggestions to improve our mentor program.

Copyright © 2009 by Corwin Press. All rights reserved. Reprinted from *Mentoring as Collaboration: Lessons From the Field for Classroom, School, and District Leaders* by Mary Ann Blank and Cheryl A. Kershaw. Thousand Oaks, CA: Corwin Press, www.corwinpress.com. Reproduction authorized only for the local school site or nonprofit organization that has purchased this book.

PAIRING MENTORS WITH BEGINNING TEACHERS: GUIDELINES

Purpose: To most successfully match mentors with new teachers

Timing: When designing the mentor program

Matching decisions should be made thoughtfully and professionally based on several factors. The essential question is this: Which mentor (or mentors) can best assist this novice in becoming an effective teacher? Often, two mentors (with specific division of duties) are better than one. In making these pairings, consider these factors:

- *Expertise.* Each mentor assigned to a new teacher should be able to provide appropriate and complementary support. Some schools only provide one mentor. Others involve more of their faculty through the second mentor role.
  - *Primary mentor.* This colleague should have expertise in the same grade or subject assignment as the novice. It is critical that the assigned mentor have the ability to coach with specific content or grade-level information to focus on instructional planning and assessment.
  - *Second mentor.* This could be a colleague at a different grade level or in a different department. This mentor assumes a more informal, less structured mentoring role—often as a committed listener and problem solver who may be able to address issues from a different perspective. In one of our high-performing schools, these mentors help coach new teachers on reflective practice in preparation for their evaluation process—by assisting them in reflecting on taped teaching segments and linking these reflections to the formal evaluation requirements.
- *Educational philosophies.* When the individuals involved are operating from different beliefs about learning and learners, conflicts are more likely. Mentoring requires time and effort on the part of the experienced teachers. Matching educational philosophies as closely as possible can avoid unnecessary tension and frustration for both the mentor and the beginning teacher.

❝──────────────── Comments From the Field ────────────────

As a protégé of a wonderful mentor, I feel strongly that successful mentoring depends on the quality of the relationship. It must be based on trust and open communication. There were times when I was very frustrated and I really didn't want anyone else to know. My mentor allowed me a safe place to "melt down" and then get back to business.

Second Year Middle School Teacher

One successful strategy we use is to assign a primary mentor (at grade level or subject area, if possible) and a secondary mentor (at a different grade and subject area, but in close proximity, if possible). The secondary mentors are designated as "professional associates" and assume a more informal but structured and purposeful role in assisting the beginning teacher. This has increased the ownership and has worked well for us!

Lead Mentor in a High School

──**❞**

- *Personalities.* While the logical advice may be to match like personalities, many outstanding relationships develop between pairings of exact opposites!
  - Some MCTs use Multiple Intelligence or other styles of assessments (i.e., Gregoric Thinking Styles, Myers-Briggs Inventories, Learning Styles, True Colors) to provide helpful information in assigning a mentor to a protégé. One positive outcome is increased awareness of the individual differences in approaches to learning.
  - Compatibility concerns are also good reasons for a second mentor. If the primary mentor is not highly compatible in terms of personalities or philosophies, it could be that the secondary mentor will provide that match.
- *Age.* While age is not the most important criterion, it is worth considering. Age-based intergenerational differences impact perceptions of the world, relationships, and work. Baby Boomers, Gen Xers, and Millennials think very differently about many aspects of their life, especially how they approach their careers. At the same time, some young mentors experience "discomfort" or "intimidation" when their protégé is older and/or has more work experience. These young mentors may need guidance in adapting their assistance to match the unique strengths of their protégés. Likewise, these protégés need to understand their responsibilities as new educators and professional learners and the importance of the relationship with their mentors.

> **❝ A Comment From the Field**
>
> Many small, rural schools also have "isolated" beginning teachers who do not have on-site access to a mentor with the same certification or who are teaching the same grade or subject. Members of our MCT have (or can find) connections to educators in other schools in the system (or even in other systems) that can provide the mentoring needed. E-mail has been a big help, but we also try to give them time to visit one another.
>
> *Small, Rural Middle School Lead Mentor* **❞**

- *Close proximity.* Pairing colleagues whose classrooms are close to each other promotes frequent contact and sharing. If neither the primary nor the secondary mentor is closely situated to the new teacher, another educator should be designated as a professional associate or "buddy" to the novice. Early in the year, many novices gain confidence and security by daily contact (and sometimes multiple daily contacts) with mentors.
- *Gender.* Again, the advice is to assign two mentors, one of the same gender, if appropriate and possible.
- ***Specialized certification needs (art, music, guidance, special education, ELL, etc.).*** These new teachers need a formal connection to a mentor with the same certification. The MCT can arrange for networking across schools in the district or e-mentoring as ways to establish these necessary professional relationships.
- ***Assigning an initial, temporary mentor.*** Many schools have found that this allows needed time to get to know the novices' personalities, interests, and other assets. The information is then used to make a *permanent* match. This works well when there are several qualified mentors for each grade.

✓ **Research to Practice Insight:** Two factors contribute most strongly to productive mentor/new teacher pairings: proximity and same grade/level or subject area!

—S. Villani, 2004

66———————————— **Comments From the Field** ————————————

Thinking in terms of generations helps you understand some of the behaviors you are seeing. So now, instead of complaining about the millenials' lack of work ethic, I realize that their way of working is just different from what I am used to. For example, our MCT was offering general planning assistance after school—which they did not appear to want. What we didn't realize it that they were collecting numerous lesson plans from various Internet sources. We came to see that what they really needed was assistance in sorting, selecting, and revising the activities so they would "fit" the needs of their students. We realize now that our coaching should focus on assuring that their planning moves beyond delivering content and "doing activities," to selecting the best learning experiences that promote student learning.

Secondary Lead Mentor

Many college students post information on the Internet without realizing the impact it might have or how easily it could be misinterpreted at some point in the future. What they post on the Internet never goes away. As new teachers, they have to be much more careful, selective, and professional in whatever they post. A similar caution should be shown in using e-mails to communicate with others.

Experienced Secondary Mentor

————————————————————————————————————— **99**

UNDERSTANDING DIFFERENCES IN MENTORS AND BEGINNING TEACHERS: GUIDELINES

Purpose: To help the MCT and mentors recognize differences in the ways experienced and new teachers approach their professional responsibilities; to promote dialogue and collaboration across the faculty; to maximize mentor/new teacher pairings; and to strengthen teacher and administrator leadership

Timing: When establishing or troubleshooting mentor/beginning teacher pairings

Use the chart (Table 7.1) as a means to open lines of communication about how generational experiences influence faculty perceptions, professional relationships, and approaches to change. Consider these factors in making mentor/beginning teacher pairings.

Table 7.1 Understanding Differences in Mentors and Beginning Teachers

Generations	Characteristics	Careers and Relationships	Professional Needs
Traditionalists (1922–1943)	• Hard-working • Persevering, even sacrificing • Willing to conform, sacrifice • Formal • Respect for authority and rules • Stable and loyal • Communicate effectively (grammar, interpersonal skills) • Financially conservative	• Organizational loyalty—typically focused on one career • Dislike conflict • Focus on what has worked in the past • Focus on vision and desired outcomes • Value and support teamwork	• Acknowledgment from others • Value of their experience and expertise • Opportunities to build relationships • Job security • Safe and secure work environments • Leadership that is direct, clear, logical, and respectful
Baby Boomers (1943–1960)	• Hard-working • Strong work ethic • People and teamwork oriented • Service-oriented • Creative and critical thinkers • Value individuality • Relationship-oriented • Strong interpersonal skills • Caring • Generally optimistic • Less financially conservative than traditionalists	• Less organizational loyalty—often change careers if needs not met • Avoid conflict • Focus on team building and involving others to solve problems • Focused on vision and desired outcomes • Admire those who succeed • Expect loyalty • Process-oriented	• Involvement • Collaboration • Opportunities to build relationships • Work environments that nurture relationships and teamwork • Job security • Opportunities to pursue individual interests • Leadership that involves stakeholders and collaboration
GenXers (1960–1980)	• Hard-working when motivated • Results-oriented • Value diversity • Independent • Informal • Can be skeptical or cynical • Self-reliant • Make "fun" a priority • Pragmatic • Adaptable • Creative • Global thinkers • Technology-oriented • Not as people-oriented as previous generations • Unintimidated by authority	• Minimal organizational loyalty • Focus on strategies to reduce stress and workload • Seek work that is personally fulfilling • Like to do things their way • Impatient with colleagues or leaders who do not see things as they do • Often adapt rather than follow rules and procedures • Often exhibit poor people or communication skills • Seek ways to make work more efficient (new technology and software)	• Control their work environment and time • Open and immediate communication with all members of the organization (regardless of position) • Diversity in the workplace and work • Opportunities to find new solutions • Career security • Technology to make work more efficient • Leadership that gets to the point and can handle what appears to be cynical behavior

(Continued)

Table 7.1   (Continued)

Generations	Characteristics	Careers and Relationships	Professional Needs
Millenials (1981–2000)	• Achievement-oriented • Tenacious • Confident • Optimistic • Socially adept • Committed to social justice and civic responsibility • Team-oriented • Creative • Protected and pampered by family • Multi-taskers • Like flexibility • Technologically adept • Like to text and email and use open source Web sites like Facebook	• Like structure and supervision • Like thinking of new solutions • Want to have their ideas accepted, despite their inexperience • Inexperienced with interpersonal conflict • Seek work that is personally fulfilling and makes a difference in society • Focus on strategies to reduce stress and workload • Value and support teamwork • Cannot imagine work without technology—and want the latest and best	• Seek mentors who help them learn their jobs • Details for required tasks • Attention and reinforcement from colleagues and superiors • Open communication with colleagues and superiors • Recognition for their contributions • The latest in technology • Lifestyle security • Leadership that is aware of their needs and fulfills them • Guidance in communicating electronically with families and community members • Use caution in posting pictures or information on the Internet that can be viewed by others (e.g., misinterpretation, permanent, non-retractable)

Sources: Data from Perkins & Hu (2007); Zemke, Raines, & Flipczak (2000).

❝———————— **A Comment From the Field** ————————

Our MCT shared this information at one of our fall forums to help us understand that on any faculty there are going to be differences of perspective and differences are OK—and even valued. This has been a good point of reference for us in working together effectively. As a matter of fact, we really have fun with it. My mentor will sometimes say, 'Miss Technology Guru, please help this Baby Boomer find what I just lost in some hidden file on my computer.'

First Year Teacher

—————————————————————————————————❞

Discussion Starters:

☞ The majority of beginning teachers are Millenials, followed by Generation Xers. Most mentors are Baby Boomers, followed by Generation Xers or Traditionalists. What do we need to consider to best encourage their involvement in our school culture?

☞ What potential obstacles might arise as a result of differing perspectives?

☞ How do we capitalize on the strengths that they bring to our school?

☞ What do we need to consider in making mentor/new teacher pairings?

☞ What specific leadership do they need from teacher leaders as well as administrators?

❝ ———————— Comments From the Field ————————

It is not fair to the new teachers (or the students) to hire them into the most challenging teaching assignments in the most difficult schools. The same is true for assigning new teachers time-consuming non-curricular assignments or inconvenient classrooms or "traveling" situations. We know they will do it—just to get the job!

Secondary Lead Mentor

Some of our new teachers seem so independent. They just don't seem to appreciate what we're trying to do for them. They always have something to do after school—and have a million reasons why they cannot stay to meet with us. Yet when they want something, they want it "right then" and expect us to drop everything we're doing to help them. The fact is, they are really talented for beginning teachers. I have to hand it to them that they are using information from the Internet and doing things we are just learning how to do. Maybe they just don't think they need our help.

Elementary Mentor

———————————————————————————— ❞

8

How to Ensure New Teachers' Commitment to Mentoring

Expectations for another key group—the new teachers—are presented for consideration and revision. New teachers need to know from the outset that they are welcomed and supported, but that they are also expected to actively and willingly participate in the mentoring process. Once MCT expectations are agreed upon, they need to be shared. One major complaint we have heard loud and clear from mentors is their frustration in working with new teachers who are not eager professional learners. Typical descriptions of these new teachers include "thinks she already knows it all," "doesn't listen to my advice—much less follow it," and "doesn't appear to think I have anything to offer." Effective mentors express major disappointment when their "help" is not valued nor appreciated. While most new teachers have a productive grasp of their roles, there are some who definitely do not. Avoid getting caught in the trap of assuming that beginning teachers will value a mentor's assistance and that they will eagerly participate in the professional development activities provided to help them. An effective preventive strategy is to overtly communicate professional learning behaviors, expected dispositions, and expectations for participation in mentor program activities by using the following **Expectations and Responsibilities for New Teachers: Checklist** and **New Teacher and Mentor Acceptance of Commitment: Sample Forms.** This conveys the expectation for productive professional learning that begins with mentoring and extends throughout the teacher's career as a member of the school's Professional Learning Community.

EXPECTATIONS AND RESPONSIBILITIES FOR NEW TEACHERS: CHECKLIST

Purpose: To clearly communicate expectations

Timing: When designing the mentor program

Review these suggested expectations for your new teachers. Identify the ones that would be appropriate and relevant for your school setting. Collectively, the purpose is to identify clear expectations.

_____ Remain committed to your role as a developing professional.

_____ Progress on and accomplish all activities in your Induction Plan, including attending and actively contributing to mentor program-sponsored professional development activities.

_____ Exhibit the effort and energy it takes to become an effective educator.

_____ Show initiative by being willing and eager to do "what needs to be done," but avoid becoming overloaded.

_____ Work collaboratively and cooperatively with your mentor and other colleagues.

_____ Value your mentor's help by requesting feedback and being receptive and responsive to it.

_____ Ask questions, listen attentively, clarify confusions, attempt to act positively on appropriate suggestions, and persist in implementing suggested actions.

_____ Provide suggestions that may improve our induction program in meeting the needs of other beginning teachers.

_____ Collaborate with your mentor and our lead mentor in productively resolving any challenges encountered.

_____ Become a self-analytic, reflective, and independent professional who can become a mentor to others.

Copyright © 2009 by Corwin Press. All rights reserved. Reprinted from _Mentoring as Collaboration: Lessons From the Field for Classroom, School, and District Leaders_ by Mary Ann Blank and Cheryl A. Kershaw. Thousand Oaks, CA: Corwin Press, www.corwinpress.com. Reproduction authorized only for the local school site or nonprofit organization that has purchased this book.

NEW TEACHER AND MENTOR ACCEPTANCE OF COMMITMENT: SAMPLE FORMS

Purpose: To help the new teacher appreciate and acknowledge his/her position as a developing professional and to commit to the related responsibilities; to help mentors fully understand and commit to their leadership roles and responsibilities.

Timing: At the beginning of the mentor/protégé relationship

Use these as samples or make any changes needed to reflect the expectations of your mentor program.

New Teacher Acceptance of Commitment

Date:

I, _____, accept and commit to work with my mentor, _____, during this school year. I have reviewed the school's expectations for me and am aware of my role as a developing professional. I am willing to expend the effort and energy it takes to become an effective educator. I will eagerly ask questions, listen attentively to responses, clarify confusions, and attempt to act positively on appropriate suggestions. I will also provide suggestions that may make our mentoring program more successful in meeting the needs of other beginning teachers. I am willing to collaborate with _____ (our lead mentor) in working through any challenges we may encounter. I also commit to attending and being an active contributor to mentor-sponsored professional development activities.

Mentor Acceptance of Commitment

Date:

I, _____, am willing to commit the time and energy necessary to serve as a mentor to _____ during this school year. I am fully aware of my responsibilities, the confidentiality I must maintain, and the roles I am to serve. I will do all I can to help the novice develop into a fully functioning professional and effective educator. I will also provide any suggestions that may make our mentoring program more successful in meeting the needs of our beginning teachers. I am also willing to collaborate with _____ (our lead mentor) in working through any challenges we may encounter.

Copyright © 2009 by Corwin Press. All rights reserved. Reprinted from *Mentoring as Collaboration: Lessons From the Field for Classroom, School, and District Leaders* by Mary Ann Blank and Cheryl A. Kershaw. Thousand Oaks, CA: Corwin Press, www.corwinpress.com. Reproduction authorized only for the local school site or nonprofit organization that has purchased this book.

9

How to Coordinate Support to New Teachers

In our complex and challenging educational world, it is becoming apparent that one mentor cannot do it all. That is, individual mentors may not have the time, energy, or expertise to meet every need the novice may have and simultaneously maintain his or her own sanity and professional obligations. Especially in schools with unstable faculties and many novice teachers, the needs of beginning teachers may require additional external assistance beyond what is provided internally by individual mentors or the Mentor Core Team. Many districts across the nation, especially those that are faced with multiple schools with consistently high teacher turnover, are adding an external level of systemwide teacher leadership to help schools provide quality support for their new faculty members.

In the most productive induction programs, levels of support range from basic to intensive, depending on the specific needs of beginning teachers (see **Framework for Levels of Mentor Support: Guidelines,** below). This means, however, that the school-based MCT should preassess their new teachers to identify their needs.

> 66 ——— **A Comment From the Field** ———
>
> I really appreciated the help of my mentors, but it became very frustrating when I had so much input and advice—I really couldn't follow it all. It was all good information, but I had too many priorities and too much to even think about!
>
> *Frustrated First-Year Teacher*
> 99

Our work has taught us that in every school, the *basic* or *minimal* level of support must be the MCT, with an individual mentor assigned as the primary mentor to each new teacher. An *expanded* level of support is the addition of internal or "in-house" support provided by trained educators who may be considered secondary mentors. These individuals may have the role of academic coach, literacy coach, or curriculum facilitator. Their job responsibilities are usually well aligned with those of mentors.

For most new teachers, the basic and expanded levels provide satisfactory support. However, in settings with a high percentage of new teachers (i.e., number of new teachers exceeds the number of high-quality mentors) or when one or several new teachers struggle on a daily basis and are not progressing at an acceptable rate with the existing mentor support, an intensive level of support is needed. At this point, external district support providers such as supervisors, retired educators, higher education faculty members, or extensively trained full-time mentors can provide the expertise and intensive daily or weekly coaching, observation, and feedback that is beyond the capacity (i.e., expertise, time, resources) of the school-based team. Collaboration between the in-house and external mentors can be facilitated by the MCT, which would then allow the external mentors to focus their help on those who need it most—the new teachers who are experiencing the most significant needs. See **Centralized Support Structure: Guidelines**, below, for a visual representation of this.

> **66 —— A Comment From the Field ——**
>
> Using the MCT to coordinate all support in our school has helped us use our resources better. Our district provides New Teacher Advisors who are an invaluable resource to our new teachers, but they can't be everywhere at once!
>
> *Middle School Administrator*
> **99**

✓ **Research to Practice Insight:** Consistency is critical when multiple support providers are mentoring. There is a real potential for "mixed messages" and perceptions of competing priorities that can lead to confusion and frustration at all levels. Coordination and communication between MCTs and external and internal mentors can assure quality and consistency in coaching, terminology, and support. School-based mentors provide contextual information about programs, strategies, and priorities to assist external support providers in their coaching efforts. External mentors provide assistance beyond the capacity of the school-based team. The beginning teachers served by their collaboration benefit from clearly focused and structured support. With coordination from the MCT, the resources provided by this expanded system can be used effectively and efficiently. The supplementary support providers can focus their skills and time where they are needed, while the individual mentors and team provide ample, high-quality support for most novices. —The Authors

---

> **66 ———————————— A Comment From the Field ————————————**
>
> We are seeing the benefits of collaborating with the school's Mentor Core Team. In some situations our case loads are too large to serve everyone well. I work with 15 schools and have about 70 new teachers that I can only see every two to three weeks. Some beginning teachers have so many needs and, to make matters worse, they often need immediate help on days that we are in other schools. We feel badly that we can't be there for them when they desperately need us. We now can confer with the MCTs and work with novices who need our help the most. This has helped increase our level of satisfaction with our jobs—and the new teachers are more satisfied, too!
>
> *District-Level External Support Provider*
> **99**

FRAMEWORK FOR LEVELS OF MENTOR SUPPORT: GUIDELINES

Purpose: To meet the support needs of beginning teachers in coordinated, consistent ways; to promote additional support from internal mentors; to allow external mentors to focus their efforts on beginning teachers with ongoing or unmet needs (as described in Table 9.1, below; for additional information on expanding mentoring support, see Fletcher & Barrett, 2004)

Timing: When designing the mentor program

Table 9.1   Framework for Levels of Mentor Support

Basic	*Expanded*	*Intensive*
Provided by Mentors & School-Based Mentor Team (MCT)	**Internal Support Providers**	**External Support Providers**
The *minimal* level of support consists of an individual mentor being assigned to each beginning teacher.	An additional level of support added to the basic level	In settings where a high percentage of novices (which exceeds the number of high-quality mentors) and/or novices struggle on a daily basis and are not progressing satisfactorily
The MCT is composed of an administrator and a team of teacher leaders representing grade levels, core content areas, and special areas (a minimum of one per school) who develop, implement, and evaluate all mentoring and support activities for beginning teachers in their school.	Trained educators who may be secondary mentors, professional associates, literacy coaches, or curriculum facilitators	Specifically trained, experienced classroom teachers or retired teachers to serve as new-teacher advisors; retired teachers; district-level supervisors; or higher education partners
Appropriate and adequate support for most beginning teachers	Generally welcomed and positive support for most beginning teachers	Needed expertise and intensive daily or weekly coaching, observation, and feedback that is beyond the capacity (i.e., expertise, time, resources) of the school-based team

CENTRALIZED SUPPORT STRUCTURE: GUIDELINES

Purpose: To coordinate the support services to teachers, as illustrated by Figure 9.1, below

Timing: When designing or strengthening the mentor program

Figure 9.1   Centralized Support Structure

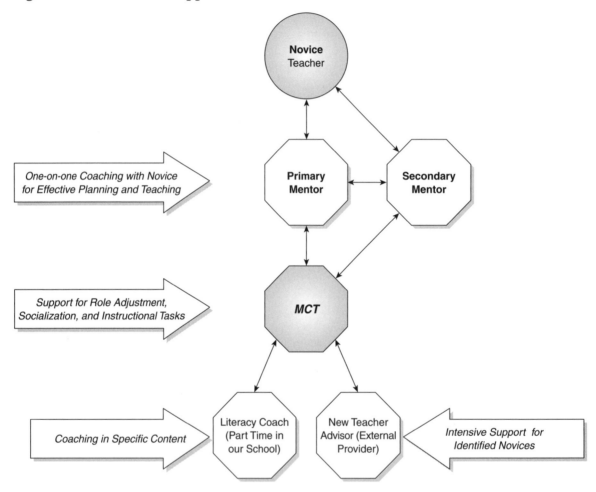

✓ **Research to Practice Insight:** The coordination provided by a school-based MCT assures that the assistance to new teachers is focused, not fragmented.

10

How to Promote Professional Learning and Schoolwide Collaboration

Attitudes and readiness for professional learning vary greatly on both individual and organizational levels. Historically, educators have expressed a variety of reasons for the negative feelings regarding their professional development experiences. The primary complaint is lack of relevance to their day-to-day teaching and their own classroom or school context. As more and more are working to develop Professional Learning Communities, school-based professional development opportunities are focused on *real*, specific needs; are well designed; involve embedded experiences that improve instruction; and capitalize on the knowledge and expertise of faculty in the school, teachers' attitudes, and perceptions about professional development change (see **Creating a School-Based Professional Sharing Structure: Example,** below). These characteristics are what currently distinguish quality professional learning from the traditional smorgasbord-type professional development (see **Aligning With Professional Development Standards: Guidelines**, below). It is also what differentiates traditional, informal teacher mentoring from purposeful, high-quality teacher mentoring experiences.

The National Staff Development Council (NSDC) provides guidance for professional learning experiences. The NSDC recommends that all professional development activities address the professional context in which the learning occurs as well as incorporate high-quality and relevant learning processes and content. The professional development opportunities provided through your mentor program should be purposefully and thoughtfully designed.

✓ **Research to Practice Insight:** Mentoring is one of the most significant forms of professional development—one that has lasting impact. Research findings suggest that the ways teachers learn to teach in their first years set the pattern for how they will continue to learn throughout their entire careers.

—Feiman-Nemser, 2001; Blank et al., 2006

ALIGNING WITH PROFESSIONAL DEVELOPMENT STANDARDS: GUIDELINES

Purpose: To ensure high-quality and pervasive professional sharing; to use as a review of recommended professional development standards; to identify strengths as well as areas that need improvement

Timing: As program is being designed and as an annual review

In order to be the productive professional learning experience mentoring must be, your program activities should be aligned with roles adapted from the NSDC standards for context, process, and content. Review the statements by identifying and discussing the level of challenge that may be encountered when implementing your program. The next step is then to identify strategies to minimize or overcome the challenges!

STEP 1:

☞ Which recommendations will be EASY for us?

☞ Which recommendations will be a CHALLENGE for us?

The Professional Development CONTEXT (i.e., the organization, system, or culture in which the new learning is implemented) **of our Mentor Program should be designed to**
- promote a school culture that is supportive of new learning;
- result in changes in classroom practice for most teachers (novices, mentors, and colleagues);
- be viewed as an essential component for achieving the purposes of the organization and as an integral part of the school's improvement plan;
- facilitate planning and learning during the school day; and
- be valued as one important Professional Learning Team in the school.

The Professional Development PROCESS (i.e., the means or the methods used for the acquisition of new knowledge and skills) **of our Mentor Program should be designed to**
- provide numerous opportunities for new (and other) teachers to acquire new knowledge and skills;
- function effectively using productive group process (e.g., decision making, communication, and teamwork);

- provide activities that are consistent with the principles of adult learning;
- provide activities that are collaborative, informal, and respectful;
- provide activities that reflect knowledge of the change process;
- find constructive solutions to the "implementation dip" that inevitably occurs;
- provide activities that are based on data regaring valued student outcomes;
- promote implementation of innovations from School Improvement Plans;
- provide activities that are comprehensive, including theory, demonstration, practice with feedback, and coaching;
- increase staff ownership through consensus decision making; and
- model effective interpersonal and collaborative skills (including regular assessment of skills and goal setting).

66 ——— A Comment From the Field ———

We have been focusing on making our school a positive place for our new teachers. What we now agree on is that every teacher—not just new ones—needs a professional support system. We are acting on our belief that effective and dedicated teachers are our school's most valuable resource.

Middle School Librarian (Member of the MCT) **99**

The Professional Development CONTENT (i.e., the actual skills and knowledge effective educators need to possess or acquire) **of our Mentor Program should be designed to**

- provide activities that address research-based and developmentally-appropriate instructional, management, and assessment practices.
- provide activities that address key research-based, best practices such as understanding the developmental and learning needs of students; establishing relationships with learners and partnerships with their families; using approaches to ensure an equitable and excellent education for all students; making curriculum and instruction connect to real-life, meaningful applications; ensuring rigor by facilitating higher level learning; enacting high expectations for all students; communicating to parents about individual student's academic progress; and assessing students in a variety of ways.

Source: National Staff Development Council, found at http://www.nsdc.org/standards/index.cfm

---

STEP 2:

☞ What strategies can we use to address the recommendations that will be CHALLENGES for us? (Be creative in brainstorming all possibilities!)

✓ **Research to Practice Insight:** Mentoring should be embedded in the work of teaching and learning—as is the case with all effective professional development. Mentoring should be purposeful, timely, comprehensive, and based on novice teachers' needs. It should focus on the everyday responsibilities, issues, and activities of teaching and learning. It should not include unrelated or excessive expectations for new teachers.

— Darling-Hammond, 2003; Feiman-Nemser, 2001

CREATING A SCHOOL-BASED PROFESSIONAL SHARING STRUCTURE: EXAMPLE

Purpose: To provide an example of a structure for professional learning that increases faculty involvement, promotes shared responsibility, and widespread commitment to supporting novice (actually all) teachers

Timing: At any appropriate point to strengthen your Mentor Program (initiating, developing, or sustaining stages)

Process Used: Based on their pre-assessments of their beginning teachers, the MCT developed a list of important topics of interest or need for their beginning teachers. They "nominated" colleagues with expertise in these areas to support the beginning teachers informally. They also included secretaries in sharing the "dos" and "don'ts" of school paperwork and procedures. In developing this "expert list," they involved everyone on the faculty in some significant way—building a community of support and validating expertise!

Result: Engaging others increases the level of professional sharing, but it also increases the performance expectations for all educators (see also **Linking MCT to School Leadership and Other PLCs: Guidelines**, below). Many educators are prepared and ready to share productive strategies, advice, and experiences. Novices (and experienced colleagues) have timely access to new learning opportunities, assistance with areas of concern, or guidance and troubleshooting. Topics that were "need-to-know information" were offered at designated after-school, on-site professional development sessions called "30-Minute Thursdays."

> 66———— **A Comment From the Field** ————
>
> Mentors are really teacher leaders who have honed their areas of expertise and who have developed effective ways to facilitate the professional learning of their colleagues—new and experienced! For many teacher leaders, this is an unfamiliar and uncomfortable role. We work hard to become effective "teachers" to adults.
>
> *Elementary Administrator* 99

Table 10.1 Expert Teams: An In-House Support Network

Lesson and Unit Planning	Classroom Mgt./Discipline	Instructional Strategies
Smith, Stewart, Jackson	Hall, Johnson, Turner	Simons, Carthage, Bagley
Cooperative Learning	**Special Education/ Individualized Instruction**	**Motivational Strategies**
Hill, Nixon, Redd	Dolen, Paul, Rider	Short, Newsom, Higley
Questioning Techniques	**Time Management and Organizational Skills**	**Paperwork—Processes and Forms**
Ott, Bell	Rivers, Townsend, Atkins	Farmer, Schott, Wilson
Creating and Using Rubrics	**Integrating Technology Instruction**	**Project-Based Learning**
Hembree, McRae	Benner, Hatch	Humphrey, Johnson
PowerPoint Presentation Smart Boards	**Issues in Urban Education**	**Teacher Evaluation Process**
Benner	Cagle, McLaughlin	Bellon, Reynolds

✓ **Research to Practice Insight:** "LINKING PIN" Organizational Structure:
A key to effective coordination is to have one member of the school leadership team also be a member of the Mentor Core Team—thus creating a LINK between the school's leadership and the MCT. A LINK should be created for every other major team or PLC with the school leadership team. —Likert, 1967

LINKING MCT TO SCHOOL LEADERSHIP AND OTHER PLCS: GUIDELINES

Purpose: To ensure coordination, communication, and efficiency of effort. Schools are complex organizations, and the complexity increases with school size. Teacher mentoring is only one of the critical "systems" in a school that must be coordinated with other organizational structures (see Figure 10.1).

Timing: When designing or strengthening a mentor program

Figure 10.1   School Leadership Team

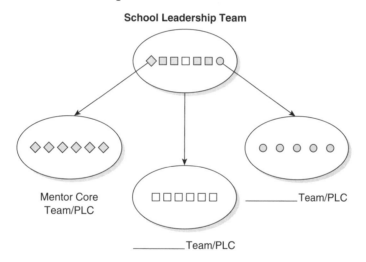

66 ──────────────── **Comments From the Field** ────────────────

After attending mentor training, our MCT shared with the entire faculty the importance of supporting one another. They then asked each teacher (novice as well as "seasoned") to identify areas of expertise that they would be comfortable teaching to all faculty. The MCT was then able to include everyone on at least one Expert Team. We have had great success with this—it's all part of our learning and growing together!

Elementary Principal

What a simple concept, but one that will make a real difference in our school. I was aware of a "disconnect," but wasn't sure how to attack it. I really didn't understand that by not having someone from the induction team on our school leadership team, we were not recognizing the impact that new teachers, and teacher turnover, has on student achievement. We weren't even discussing it.

High School Administrator

──**99**

11

How to Provide Time, Resources, and Support for Mentoring

Making decisions related to time, other resources, and financial support is important when designing your mentor program. A productive mentor program requires resources to fulfill its purpose and potential. We suggest that it is the responsibility of school-level and district-level administrators to provide the time and other necessary resources and support for their priority programs (see **Expectations and Responsibilities for School District Administrators: Checklist**, below). School-level administrators can provide some of the necessary resources, but to fully fund the work of the mentor program, new policies, external expertise, and assistance may often be necessary. Each school should have the flexibility to design and implement its program according to needs, but district-level guidelines, policy, and financial support should be provided to initiate, grow, and sustain programs.

✔ **Research to Practice Insight:** In our mentor workshops, the most often identified barrier to productive mentoring is time. In schools, time is probably the most valued resource—and, there never seems to be enough of it! But, finding—or making—time to mentor is necessary. Doing mentoring right is critical—and, quality mentoring requires time.

TIME REQUIREMENTS

- Mentor Core Team should meet on a regular basis. Generally, the meetings are more frequent at the beginning of the year (weekly or twice monthly) and become less frequent (monthly) as the year progresses. Some MCTs like the idea of a "retreat" prior to school start.
- MCT-sponsored events for socialization or professional development require time throughout the year of the mentors, faculty, and the new teachers involved.
- Individual mentors must have regularly scheduled and dedicated time to plan and confer with their protégés, to observe and give feedback, to model lessons and debrief with them, and so on (see **Finding or Creating Time to Mentor: Guidelines**, below).
- New teachers need regularly scheduled time to collaborate with mentors on plans, to interpret assessment data, to make initial grouping decisions, to observe mentor or other teachers and debrief observations. They typically need more time during their first few months on the job.

✓ **Research to Practice Insight:** Comprehensive induction programs should include accommodations in terms of new teacher work load, numbers of preparations, extracurricular duties, etc. The benefits of new teacher learning and professional growth are realized immediately and in the longer term. When new teachers are given quality time and support to develop their knowledge of the subjects taught and skill in reaching their students, the benefits in student learning can be realized. —A. Villar, 2005

MONETARY (AND NONMONETARY) REQUIREMENTS

- Purchases (materials, supplies, refreshments, etc.) for MCT development and/or ongoing activities (including money for Welcome Baskets; a New Teacher Luncheon; materials for the professional library; materials for professional development activities; materials to create New Teacher Handbook; payment for substitute teachers to allow planning, observing, and conferencing, etc.).

✓ **Research to Practice Insight:** Some teams have developed formulas based on the number of new teachers ($50–$100 per novice). Develop guidelines for the use of the money, and keep careful records for both documentation and future planning. There are many appropriate uses, but some typically produce a greater impact than others. For example, many new teams use their funds for "welcome baskets" and luncheons. As the teams become more mature, they often gather donations for the welcome baskets and use their funds to pay for substitute teachers so that important mentor activities can occur (e.g., observations, planning, conferencing). Other effective uses of funds include honorariums paid to teachers in the school (mentors and non-mentors) who conduct professional development sessions and materials for the professional library. Refreshments are always appreciated and, in many settings, seem to be "required"! —The Authors

- Compensation for mentors. Compensation to assigned mentors is another decision point (at the school and/or system level). While some educators' advice is to avoid paying individuals serving as mentors, others feel that mentors should be financially rewarded for the professional duties they perform outside normal school hours. If there is to be remuneration, Villani (2004) suggests that it could be a negotiated part of a teachers' contract. Some programs do compensate mentors with salary (for full- or part-time work), stipends, additional release time for professional development, money to attend conferences, reduction of nonclassroom duties, and additional personal leave. We leave this decision to the educators who know the context best.
- Get creative in identifying nonmonetary ways to compensate mentors. Nonmonetary compensation could be "time off" (an "early out" with coverage by an administrator), unscheduled in-service credit, extra duties reduced or eliminated, donated coupons, or complimentary dinners at local restaurants, and so on. Finally, maintain good relationships with adopters and PTO or whoever might respond positively to requests for goodies and funds to support mentoring.

66 ——————————————— **Comments From the Field** ———————————————

We like to have our mentors and mentees work together for one or two days before the year begins. We then compensate their time by giving them hours toward their required professional development credit.

Instructional Supervisor of a Small Rural County School System

Since I realized that mentoring should have a higher priority in our school improvement plan, I'm amazed at how much more effective and efficient our program is. Fewer teachers are leaving us after their first couple of years of teaching. More important, we're seeing the results of our efforts in student achievement gains. Our beginning teachers are teaching more like their mentors . . . far earlier than they used to. I know that we cannot say that any one initiative has made this happen. But, I believe that what we have accomplished by linking mentoring to achievement (both in our thinking and in our organizational structure) is certainly a big part of the equation.

High School Administrator

99

FINDING OR CREATING TIME TO MENTOR: GUIDELINES

Purpose: To increase Mentor/New Teacher opportunities to collaborate

Timing: Throughout the mentoring experience

Requires personal commitment:
- Communicate electronically—exchange e-mail addresses immediately.
- Schedule "sunrise" breakfasts away from the school or "social hour" informal gatherings after school.
- Plan ahead and make your own moments. Arrange for supervisory assistance (instructional assistants, administrators, student teachers, interns, parents) when classes are combined (as with reading buddies, tutoring time, enrichment, and special activities). Mentor and novice remain in the room, but are occupied in planning and conferencing.
- During the mentor's planning time, find a creative but educationally sound way for novice teachers' students to be supervised and engaged in learning.
- During the novice's planning time, find a creative but educationally sound way for mentoring teacher's students to be supervised and engaged in learning.
- If facilities permit, engage in true team teaching and readjust schedules flexibly to meet mentoring needs.
- Barter with grade-level or subject area colleagues to encourage them to voluntarily take one class or lesson for new teachers one or two hours per week for additional collaborative planning time at the beginning of the school year.
- Encourage the novice to enroll in a quality online mentor site for new teachers. The advice may be generic, but the *live* mentor could reinforce specifics and details to make it work in the school setting.
- Make better use of regularly scheduled planning times, faculty meetings, and other professional development times. Eliminate time wasters. Reduce or eliminate "*administrativia*" and information sessions (sharing information in more effective ways). Use some amount of time focused on targeted teaching and learning priorities.

Requires supportive colleagues:
- Collaborate with novice and other colleagues during team meetings and planning times. Hopefully, schedules have been creatively and effectively rearranged for common planning times.

Requires approval:
- In many schools and districts, general duties are spread evenly among all faculty members (bus, recess, etc.). Suggest that the duties of mentoring should relieve mentors and novices from duties that restrict their opportunities to collaborate.
- Give unscheduled in-service credit (doesn't create more time, but does make us feel better!).

❝——— A Comment From the Field ———

One way I have found time to mentor is to do my work while my protégé is doing hers. We sit together while we grade papers, create lesson plans, or design rubrics. It allows for timely and spontaneous mentoring and we often create samples that we can share with others.

Experienced Mentor

❞

- Provide early release days. Lengthen school day on four days and allow early release on one day.
- If any professional development times are devoted to school improvement priorities, mentoring and induction activities should qualify!
- Establish a bank or "pool" of 30–40 days/year for teachers to tap into when they participate in agreed-upon mentoring responsibilities, or other professional development work.

Requires $$$:
- Hire substitute teachers to rotate through the day to free teachers to do demonstration lessons, observations, conferencing, and planning. Prior planning for an enrichment activity (or other engaging lessons that are not focused on new learning) keeps the time productive for the students. Another idea is to cover the new teacher's class for the first two to three days of their first semester so that focused, intentional observations of master teachers can occur.
- Consider hiring qualified retired teachers as replacement teachers. Provide salary and proportionate benefits.
- Organize a retreat (with contributions from benefactors) to allow mentors and novices to get to know each other in an informal setting. This could involve all mentors and novices at one time or could be scheduled by selected groups if your numbers are too large to facilitate interaction.

❝━━━━━━━━━━━━━━━━━ A Comment From the Field ━━━━━━━━━━━━━━━━━

We decided to have systemwide, grade-level (or subject-area) professional development sessions for mentors and their protégés. These were held fairly early in the school year. Their task was to work from the system's guides (and school calendars) to pace their curriculum. We kept it relaxed and productive. It was a huge success. They accomplished so much, and they loved the networking opportunities.

Supervisor of Professional Development of a Large Metropolitan District

━━━❞

EXPECTATIONS AND RESPONSIBILITIES FOR SCHOOL DISTRICT ADMINISTRATORS: CHECKLIST

Purpose: To clearly communicate expectations

Timing: When designing the mentor program

Review these suggested expectations for central office administrator(s) who are responsible for the mentor program. Identify the ones that would be appropriate and relevant for your district setting. Collectively, the purpose is to identify clear expectations.

_____ Serve as an advocate for mentoring and for all beginning teachers.

_____ Provide orientation and any needed system-level professional development for beginning teachers.

_____ Collaborate with administrators and colleagues to ensure widespread ownership of the mentor program.

_____ Provide adequate resources (including time) and support to Mentor Core Teams.

_____ Provide assistance to Mentor Core Teams to ensure their progress in designing, implementing, and sustaining their programs.

_____ Ensure the quality of each mentor program by reviewing assessment data generated by each team, providing feedback and consultation to teams, and monitoring the results achieved by the mentor programs.

_____ Incorporate mentoring activities, mentors, and MCTs in Comprehensive School System Improvement Plan and monitor all elements of the programs.

_____ Maintain regular communication with Mentor Core Teams (through the Lead Mentors) and promote collaboration across all teams in the district.

_____ Provide (or facilitate planning and delivery of) initial and ongoing Professional Development sessions for mentors during the year to promote networking and program development.

_____ Provide regular updates about mentoring activities and outcomes to the system or district leadership.

Copyright © 2009 by Corwin Press. All rights reserved. Reprinted from *Mentoring as Collaboration: Lessons From the Field for Classroom, School, and District Leaders* by Mary Ann Blank and Cheryl A. Kershaw. Thousand Oaks, CA: Corwin Press, www.corwinpress.com. Reproduction authorized only for the local school site or nonprofit organization that has purchased this book.

Part III

Implementing Your Teacher Mentoring Program

Being a mentor is one of the finest forms of teacher leadership. Excellent teachers seek ways to continue to grow as educators, but many do not want to become administrators—which traditionally has been the major route to job enrichment and increased professional status. Educational leaders and researchers are advocating for increased leadership capacity in schools. They are seeing that promoting the professional learning of mentors is one significant way to "grow" a new level of strong school leaders. Individual mentors acting one-on-one with new teachers produce significant results in terms of transforming them into competent, proficient, and even expert teachers. The assistance mentors provide shapes the ways protégés attend to the needs of their current students and their many future students. What always becomes clear to mentors is that serving in the various teacher leadership roles also significantly and positively changes them. The ways mentors think and talk about teaching and how they go about meeting the learning needs of students are substantially enhanced.

> **" A Comment From the Field "**
>
> I have been a classroom teacher for six years and have wanted to become a mentor for some time. My mentor got me off to a great start, and we are still really close friends. Even now when I need advice, I call her. Being asked to become a mentor is a real thrill for me. I want to mentor others the way I was mentored. It is also an honor to be recognized as a teacher leader in our school. Now, I need to follow my mentor's model and become an excellent mentor myself.
>
> *New Mentor*

✓ **Research to Practice Insight:** Mentoring develops leadership capacity. Our research supports that of others (Lambert, 2003; Moir & Bloom, 2003). It underscores our belief that mentoring does promote teacher leadership in schools. In our experience, veteran teachers become more effective in their instruction, more confident in their expertise, and more secure with their "outside the classroom" leadership responsibilities. This highlights the obvious and significant two-way benefit to mentoring—protégés learn from mentors and vice versa. Along with their enthusiasm and energy, many novices bring innovative teaching strategies, technology, and other skills.

As was discussed earlier, getting the "right" educators to serve as mentors is essential. Now, when implementing your mentor program, it is equally important for mentors to fully understand the many roles they play in successfully inducting new colleagues into the profession. We view teacher leaders who are mentors as fulfilling the following roles:

- **A Mentor is a Leader** providing transformational leadership in the grade, department, school and/or district, and also in professional organizations; contributing to professional growth activities; showing care and skill in developing the talents and strengths of adults and children; contributing to the school as a learning community.
- **A Mentor is a Professional Role Model** possessing strong expertise in content, curriculum, and instruction as well as in communicating and developing relationships with others; exhibiting productive cooperative skills in collaborating with team members.
- **A Mentor is a Liaison, Facilitator, and Relationship Builder**—a recognized leader with a positive reputation within the school community; is knowledgeable about a school's traditions and history and can create connections to others (colleagues, community members); is constantly seeking opportunities and experiences for new teachers.
- **A Mentor is a Supporter** who serves as an accepting, empathetic, and nonjudgmental listener; is an encourager and promoter of continuous improvement; provides a safety net and always remains a constant, committed, and trusted confidant.
- **A Mentor is a Coach** with experience and expertise in observing instruction and providing constructive feedback; is able to orient and coach the protégé in preparation for the formal teacher evaluation, but never evaluate—**evaluation is the responsibility of the administrator;** is knowledgeable about standards, policies, and politics; takes calculated risks in trying innovative strategies to meet students' needs; exhibits lifelong learning both personally and professionally.

Implement your teacher mentor program with these significant support roles and goals in mind. If any of the items numbered 10–14 on the **Getting Started: Teacher Mentor Program Components Self-Assessment** (see Chapter 2) were rated as *Areas to Strengthen,* then following *How To* guidelines will serve as a catalyst for site-specific decisions by members of the MCT. Use the *Resources* as they are or adapt them to fit with your program and/or the needs of your new teachers and mentors.

✔ **Research to Practice Insight:** Every child deserves to experience the highest quality instruction. When novices are mentored in productive ways, they develop effective teaching practices faster, have opportunities to problem-solve with their mentoring colleagues, and have a more in-depth understanding of how to work with students and families in their particular school, grade level, and/or content area context to promote student learning.

—The Authors

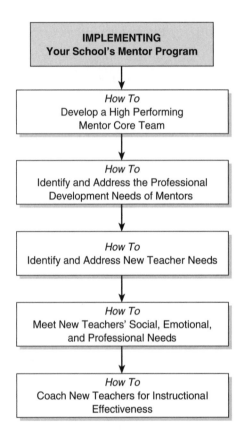

12

How to Develop a High-Performing MCT

Collaboration and teamwork are becoming increasingly important for all educators. But, not all adults *appear* to know how to be effective team members. Productive team behaviors and efficient collaboration can be developed, but they usually don't just happen. High-performing teams work to continuously improve. Decisions about "rules to live by" and procedures, made proactively, can reduce confusion, poor decision making, and professional conflicts when and if problems or barriers arise. Presented here are suggested **MCT Operational Guidelines and Procedures** for discussion by the Mentor Core Team from which your program procedures should evolve.

- **Create the Team's "Rules."** In an effort to ensure that human interactions and encounters are supportive and productive, it is important to create "rules," or codes of conduct everyone agrees to follow. Participating in developing the expectations and being committed to them make for positive relationships and forward progress. The "rules" are intended to help manage agreement as well as disagreement. Having and following adopted rules make dealing with any challenging situations more constructive.
- **Decide on Meeting Dates and Times.** Include these dates on the school's

66 ——— A Comment From the Field ———

We found that putting our MCT meeting dates *on* the school calendar before our year began was a key to our sustaining momentum. In previous years, with our informal arrangement, we had great intentions and a lot of enthusiasm, but just did not follow through on our plans. Some other pressing issue always came up. Now, with regular meetings, agendas, and specific responsibilities, we stay on track and get our plans accomplished!

Veteran Middle School Mentor

99

calendar. More frequent meetings are usually required earlier in the year. As dates for schoolwide mentoring activities are identified, add them to the calendar.

- **Adopt or Adapt Constructive Models for Decision Making and Problem Solving (see Decision Making: Guidelines and Problem Solving: Guidelines,** below). Marzano (2007) has synthesized research in the areas of decision making and problem solving and has provided models that can be adapted to school and district challenges. A side benefit of using these models is that mentors (and new teachers) begin using them in their own classrooms!

- **Develop and Use Appropriate Meeting Agenda and Protocols.** Be consistent in the use of these tools to stay on topic and operate within established time frames. Use (or revise) the provided agenda, and remember to summarize minutes, share decisions, and communicate with others in a variety of ways.

- **Create a Yearly Plan for Mentoring Activities.** Provided below as a guide for planning is **Annual Mentoring Activities: A Checklist.** Use it and **Determining New Teachers' Needs: Self-Assessment** (see page xx) as starting points for selecting *timely* activities for specific time frames (i.e., grading periods, semester). It is helpful to view support for new teachers as a continuum, starting with personal and emotional support, expanding to include general and specific task- or problem-focused support, and, ideally, promoting the novice's capacity for critical self-reflection on teaching practice. Each type of support serves a different purpose, and, in this model, each type can be provided by either individual mentors (internal or external) or the Mentor Core Team (MCT). Most MCTs accept responsibility for providing much of the generalized support—mainly focusing on helping novices feel welcomed, valued, and knowledgeable about general procedures, policies, and resources, including parents and the community. The assigned mentors are then able to focus more on specific instructional issues and promote sound pedagogical thinking and reflective practice. These two groups, MCTs and mentors, are able to meet the needs of most novices. But, as described earlier, in especially high-need situations, additional support providers, in-school specialists (curriculum facilitators, literacy coaches, etc.) and/or specially trained mentors external to the school can then provide the more intensive, situation-specific, one-on-one coaching, modeling, and observing.

- **Ensure Confidentiality of Information Shared in MCT Meetings.** Confidentiality is critical in establishing and maintaining positive, trusting relationships with new teachers. Information is confidential and should only be shared with others on a *need-to-know* basis. For mentors and MCT members to do their job, they need access to necessary information about the progress of new teachers. This information should only be used to design appropriate measures that will ensure continued growth and support. Furthermore, each individual mentor has a responsibility to his/ her assigned new teacher and to the mentor team. To maintain trust and open lines of communication, the mentor must not divulge any information

> **" ——— A Comment From the Field ———**
>
> In our mentor meetings, when we get into discussions requiring confidentiality, one of us will simply say, "What is said here, stays here."
>
> *Member of an Elementary MCT*
>
> **"**

about the new teacher's performance or competence to others—neither colleagues nor administrator.

Develop procedures for corrective action to maintain a proactive position—and hope it is never needed (see **Procedures for Corrective Action: Guidelines**, below). When a protégé is not able or not willing to live up to expectations, it is a serious disappointment to the mentor. What is important to keep in mind is that not all new teachers have the requisite level of professional knowledge, skill, or dispositions to be effective teachers. A small percentage of new teachers may exhibit a range of ineffective instructional skills, questionable actions, personal qualities, or unethical behaviors. In addition, due to many personal factors, performing at a marginal level can occur at many possible points in one's professional career. But regardless of when it occurs, corrective action must be taken. A mentor who has done everything possible to support and strengthen a new teacher should be acknowledged as doing the right thing for all the potential students who would have been negatively influenced or even harmed by this individual.

It is important to maintain positive assumptions about the capabilities and motivation of new teachers throughout the mentorship. If, however, a new teacher is not satisfactorily fulfilling the expectations identified in his or her individualized induction plan, teacher contract, or **New Teacher Acceptance of Commitment**, corrective action is required. If corrective action is needed, it becomes the responsibility of the administrator, not the mentor. Mentors could alert principals of the need for more direct and close supervision of the new teacher, but they maintain confidentiality by not sharing specific details or information.

> 66——— **A Comment From the Field** ———
>
> Regarding confidentiality—it's tricky! The way our MCT operates, if unprofessional behavior is exhibited or if an inappropriate situation develops that warrants administrative awareness, the mentor consults with the MCT about how to proceed. In many instances, the administrator allows the team to work on its own to identify the support or advice needed. But, if administrative assistance is needed, I, as the Lead Mentor, alert the administrator to the fact that the beginning teacher needs his/her assistance, but I do not share the details of a confidential situation.
>
> *High School Lead Mentor* 99

✔ **Research to Practice Insight:** As university teacher educators, we feel strongly that it is the responsibility of the teacher preparation program to identify and provide feedback to our candidates who exhibit marginal personal behaviors. We evaluate preservice teachers on their dispositions in every course. But, even with that process, early detection of inappropriate candidates isn't always the result. In addition, many programs require only a limited student teaching experience. Some of the incompetent or unprofessional behaviors that may develop later with increased responsibilities are not evident at this stage of development. Full-time teaching involves classroom-related as well as whole-school-related responsibilities. These duties require extreme skill in multi-tasking and relating to others (children and adults) as well as a strong work ethic and commitment to doing whatever it takes.

—The Authors

DECISION MAKING: GUIDELINES

Purpose: Use to make decisions that require choosing one alternative from several possibilities based upon how well the alternatives fulfill specific criteria. The following decision-making guidelines can be applied to academic, personal, and social situations and are especially helpful when the best alternative is not readily apparent (Marzano, Pickering, Arredondo, Blackburn, Brandt, & Moffett, 1997).

Timing: When needed.

Following a clearly defined process allows decision makers to engage in high-level analysis, to assign priorities to outcomes, and to learn a model that is an effective teaching tool that can be readily applied in the classroom. All models answer the essential questions:

> ☞ "What is the best way to . . . ?"
>
> ☞ "Which of these is the most suitable way to . . . ?"
>
> ☞ "Which is the best course of action?"

Steps:
- Formulate a decision question. Phrase it in a way that reflects decision making.
- Identify the choices or alternatives for consideration. Identify as many viable options as you feel are necessary. It could be that some investigation should take place to determine if all options are viable or if all good options have been identified before the actual decision making is applied.
- Identify criteria important to a good decision—as many criteria as you feel are critical. This will help the decision makers feel more comfortable and have more understanding about the relative importance of desired outcomes.
- Select the most appropriate alternative—the decision is made.
- At this point, a quantifying process may occur. Even though the decision has been made, it is still appropriate to "rethink" the process.
  - o Were the options the best ones?
  - o Were the criteria the critical ones?
  - o If a quantifying process was applied, were the importance values and the fit scores applied correctly?
  - o Additional questions: Is this a decision that is aligned with our vision? Is this a decision that we will be able to carry out (one that is realistic and feasible)?
  - o Will it produce positive results?

Considerations about making collaborative decisions:
- Is this a decision that should be arrived at through a collaborative process?
- Or is this a decision that requires a quick "yes" or "no" and is a clear-cut case?

- Is this a decision that is significant enough to warrant the time and effort collaboration requires?
- Is this a decision that those involved have the expertise (and information) to make?
- Is this a decision that we have the responsibility and the authority to decide?

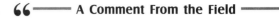

66 ——— **A Comment From the Field** ———

Our MCT judges the effectiveness of our decisions on [this question]: "Is this the best action for our students?" And then, "Is this the best action for our new teachers?"

Lead Mentor

99

PROBLEM SOLVING: GUIDELINES

Purpose: Use a process for problem solving when facing obstacles or conditions that are keeping mentors or the MCT from achieving a goal or desired outcomes. The process involves identifying the goal or desired outcome, the constraints or obstacles that are creating the problem, and a variety of possible solutions (Marzano et al., 1997).

Timing: When needed

Problem-solving models address the following essential questions:

> ☞ "What is the problem?" "Why is it a problem?"
>
> ☞ "What are the issues that are keeping the problem from being resolved?"
>
> ☞ "How can we overcome the obstacles, constraints, or conditions?"
>
> ☞ "How do we reach our goal but still address the obstacles, constraints, or conditions?"

Steps:
- Specify a goal.
  - o What is it that is hoped to be accomplished?
- Identify the constraints or limiting conditions.
  - o What is getting in the way of achieving the goal?
  - o What are the "givens" in the situation?
- Identify alternative ways to solve the problem.
  - o Review problem-solving strategies—select one or several promising ones.
- Select a solution and try it out.
  - o It may be that the solution itself is fairly complex or would require several steps.
  - o Make a plan as to how best to implement the solution.
- Evaluate the effectiveness of the solution. Questions to answer include the following:
  - o Did the solution accomplish the goal satisfactorily?
  - o Did the solution adequately accommodate the constraints?
  - o Is the solution one that is consistent with our vision?
  - o Is the solution feasible and realistic in terms of resources?

Considerations:

- It is important to designate the length of the trial period.
    o Identify a date for reviewing the effects of the trial solution.
- It is before a solution is implemented that one must think about how its success will be determined.
    o What will be the indicators of success?
    o How will you know?
    o What data or information will you need to collect, and how?
- This may seem like a laborious process, but disagreements and hurt feelings can be avoided if these steps are followed. The determination about the solution will be made based on data rather than on intuition or feelings.

ANNUAL MENTORING ACTIVITIES: CHECKLIST

Purpose: For the MCT to use as a planning resource to guide the selection of timely and need based mentor support

Timing: Throughout the year

The following are suggested school-based mentoring activities. They are arranged by time frames—when new teachers are hired, before the opening of school, days before school opens, or during the school year. In addition, the responsibility for accomplishing the activities has been designated as either an activity that would best be accomplished by the MCT or by the assigned mentor—and, in some cases, both. Select the most appropriate activities to meet your school's needs. Add your own creative ideas! Use the "P" column to designate what has been implemented.

Table 12.1 Mentoring Activities Yearly Checklist

Suggested MCT and Mentor Activities	*Mentor Core Team*	✓	*Individual Mentors*	✓
Prior to the Opening of School				
Incorporate an overview of the mentor program and expectations of mentors and beginning teachers into the interview process for hiring new teachers.	X			
Hold an orientation or informal get together to allow new teachers to meet school administrators and mentors, tour the building, and/or meet the staff.	X		X	
Contact central office personnel for details about district-wide meetings planned for beginning teachers.	X			
Prepare pre-assessment forms for beginning teachers.	X			
Develop materials for the opening of school (welcome baskets, staff directory/photo directory, school and district meeting schedules, district policies, opening of school forms).	X			
Develop or revise materials for mentors (handbooks, policies and procedures, rosters, contact information).	X			

	Mentor Core Team	✓	Individual Mentors	✓
Communicate informally with beginning teachers.				
Administer the needs assessments and analyze the information.			X	
Share an overview of the school and a typical school year.			X	
Provide the new teacher with textbooks and instructional materials.	X		X	
Help the new teacher set up the classroom/find materials or supplies.			X	
Encourage questions about any expectations or procedures that are unclear.	X		X	
Develop mentor/new teacher action plans tailored to the new teacher's needs.	X		X	
Report Mentor Core Team meetings and activities in school leadership meetings.	X			
Include copies of Mentor Core Team materials in school improvement documentation.	X			
Other				
The First Weeks of School				
Introduce the new teacher to • grade-level and/or department members; • guidance counselors, attendance personnel, special areas teachers; • support staff (secretaries, bookkeeper, cafeteria personnel, custodians, and security guards); and/or • parents and parent leaders in the school.				
Encourage the new teacher to make introductory calls to parents.			X	
Help set up the classroom and find materials and supplies.	X		X	
Show the beginning teacher where equipment is located and how to use it.	X		X	
Demonstrate how to complete forms, documents, and recordkeeping required during the first few weeks of school (bookkeeping, enrollment forms, grade books, plan books).	X		X	
Explain or review school and district policies (substitutes, student tardies and absences, office referrals, food).	X		X	
Introduce beginning teachers to the school community (tours, community mapping, resources available).	X		X	
Plan informal time to talk (social gatherings, lunch, coffee).			X	
Touch base regularly (in the beginning teacher's classroom, if possible).			X	
Write brief notes to acknowledge successes and challenges.			X	
Share stories about your own "journey" as a new teacher.			X	

(Continued)

Table 12.1   (Continued)

	Mentor Core Team	✓	Individual Mentors	✓
Schedule time to discuss topics identified as high need (mentors on an individual basis and/or Mentor Core Teams through regularly scheduled meetings): • Planning daily instruction; • Long-range planning (identifying "teachable days," pacing guides, unit planning); • Classroom management strategies; • Assessing student learning (whole class, subgroups, types of assessments and their best use); • School policies and procedures (homework, make-up work, absences/tardies, office referrals, record keeping); • Required teacher evaluation procedures; and/or • Establishing positive relationships with families (conferences, introductory telephone calls).	X		X	
Help prepare for the first meetings with parents (open house, parent conferences, conference related to a student problem).			X	
Discuss required optional professional development.			X	
Share systemwide publications (newsletters, etc.).			X	
Other				
First Semester				
Continue to "drop in" and share stories, successes, and challenges.			X	
Continue to address issues, problems, or concerns raised by the new teacher. Focus on building autonomy and self-confidence.			X	
Review current needs for curriculum materials and resources.			X	
Suggest limiting the amount of extracurricular involvement to a manageable level.			X	
Discuss balancing teaching and personal or family responsibilities.			X	
Observe each other teaching and reflect. Be specific in identifying needs and giving feedback.			X	
Conduct a preobservation conference even if it is not possible to observe the lesson being taught—and reflect with the new teacher on actual versus expected outcomes.			X	
Arrange for new teachers to be able to observe other teachers teaching—especially those with skills in the new teacher's area(s) of need or interest.	X		X	
Provide leadership on how to work effectively on school teams or committees.			X	
Schedule professional development sessions—or individual conferences—to discuss areas of identified need: • Progress with "grading"; • Challenging students at all ability levels; • Student motivation; • Classroom management/discipline; • Teacher evaluation process; and/or • Procedures for ending the first semester/beginning second.	X		X	

	Mentor Core Team	✓	Individual Mentors	✓
Hold "Brown Bag Lunches," "Early Riser Breakfasts," or "Thirty-Minute After-School Sessions" to address timely topics (Preparing for Parent Conferences or any of the discussion topics) or to discuss appropriate research-based strategies.	X			
Share resources for professional development (teacher center, local university, professional books, video libraries).	X		X	
Check in-service publications for appropriate professional development opportunities targeted to specific needs.	X		X	
Schedule substitutes to release mentors and beginning teachers to observe and conference (multiple pairs per day).	X			
Observe each other teaching, reflect, and provide concrete feedback.			X	
Arrange for new teachers to be able to observe other teachers teaching.	X		X	
Arrange for systemwide mentor support if the beginning teacher is having difficulties beyond the capacity of the school-based team (time or expertise).	X			
Send short informal notes of reinforcement and support.			X	
Plan Mentor Core Team activities for the second semester.	X			
Other				
Opening of Second Semester				
Review the new teacher's Induction Plan.			X	
Reflect on and acknowledge successes to date.			X	
Continue to address issues, problems, or concerns raised by the new teacher. Focus on building autonomy and self-confidence.			X	
Have the new teacher self-evaluate growth experiences from the first semester and discuss "next steps."			X	
Revisit planning discussion and identify strategies to maximize instructional time for the second semester.			X	
Share vacation schedules, testing dates, and other pertinent information that impact short- and long-term planning decisions.	X		X	
Share pacing guides and long-range planning for new content.			X	
Help with evaluation timetables, required paperwork, and expectations.	X		X	
Assess new teachers' perceptions of the quality of their support during the first semester. (See formative assessments and use the data to refine support for second semester and future beginning-of-the-year planning.)	X			
Other				
Second Semester				
Continue regular visits and dialogue.			X	

(Continued)

Table 12.1   (Continued)

	Mentor Core Team	✓	Individual Mentors	✓
Continue to address issues, problems, or concerns raised by the new teacher. Focus on building autonomy and self-confidence.			X	
Schedule time to periodically reflect on the teacher evaluation process.			X	
Continue forums or informal discussions on topics of need or interest: • Addressing the needs of students at all ability levels; • Using multiple, research-based strategies for instruction and assessment; • Using disaggregated data to understand the impact of teaching on learning; • Modifications and accommodations for students with special needs; • Problem- or project-based learning; • Performance assessments; and/or • Building positive relationships among students and teachers.	X		X	
Review the new teacher's Induction Plan and share resources where needed.	X		X	
Continue informal communications. (Notes are always welcomed!)			X	
Arrange for new teachers to be able to observe other teachers teaching.	X		X	
Involve the new teacher in sharing his/her expertise with others (professional development sessions, informal sessions).	X		X	
Talk about the use of community resources (guest speakers, field trips, business or agency support).			X	
Share pertinent research and professional journals.			X	
Discuss professional organizations.			X	
Plan a real (visible) celebration for the completion of the first year.	X			
Review procedures for ending the school year.	X		X	
Communicate with the principal about individual and Mentor Core Team activities.	X			
Other				
Closing of School				
Have all new teachers complete the Novice Teacher Summative Assessment.	X			
Have all mentors complete Mentor Teacher Summative Assessment.	X			
Continue to focus on new teacher's autonomy, self-confidence, and self-direction.			X	
Engage in reflection—"What was learned this year that will guide planning and teaching next year?" Revise activities and goals for next year.	X		X	
Recognize contributions and accomplishments and CELEBRATE!!	X		X	
Other				

Copyright © 2009 by Corwin Press. All rights reserved. Reprinted from *Mentoring as Collaboration:Lessons From the Field for Classroom, School, and District Leaders* by Mary Ann Blank and Cheryl A. Kershaw. Thousand Oaks, CA: Corwin Press, www.corwinpress.com. Reproduction authorized only for the local school site or nonprofit organization that has purchased this book.

✓ **Research to Practice Insight:** "Work smart"—Create mentor resources throughout the year. As mentoring events are implemented, try to "capture" important information in some way (videotape, pictures, samples, etc.) to share on the school's Web site, in subsequent years or at later points in the year. This is especially important during the developing years of your program. Many MCTs admit that they do a good job of giving information to novices who are hired in time for the beginning of school administrative days, but are not as good at providing information to those hired after school begins or at a change of semester. Having their opening welcome and orientation sessions on videotape or the Web site would be of tremendous help to new teachers who are hired late in the year or others who may simply elect to review them.

PROCEDURES FOR CORRECTIVE ACTION: GUIDELINES

Purpose: For the MCT to use when preventive measures have not worked; use as a model for developing procedures that fit your context.

Timing: When needed

In rare cases, extreme problems arise that are beyond the typical expectations and capacity of mentors. For example,

- if unethical behavior is exhibited, problem solving is not an option. The new teacher is dealt with according to established due process.
- if the behaviors are of a minor nature and deemed "remedial," the administrator engages in "problem understanding," which should lead to some possible productive solutions.
  - ○ The first steps are to reiterate the expectations and provide opportunities for clarification. It could be that expectations were misunderstood and that reiteration is all that was required.
  - ○ If the situation requires further action, examine the conditions that could be getting in the way of the new teacher's living up to expectations. Adjustments could be made, or additional guidance may provide the appropriate adjustment. If corrective

66 ——— A Comment From the Field ———

In my work with mentoring, I find that balancing my own work and life responsibilities with mentoring my protégé [is extremely] challenging. I've learned to set boundaries and be proactive in scheduling times for us to meet. Having times set in advance allows me to take care of my teaching responsibilities ahead of time so I can give attention to my protégé. I've also learned to accomplish some of my teaching tasks while being a model for the new teacher. I'm creating my newsletter while she is also creating hers. I'm filling in progress reports while she is also filling in hers. And then there are those unexpected, unpredicted events that require immediate consultation. I do my best to give several minutes to identify short-term solutions to "put out the fire," then set a time for a more extended conversation about longer-term or preventive solutions.

Experienced Mentor

99

action does not result in timely and positive resolution, the administrator should follow through on the system's teacher evaluation process. The mentor is still available for some *reasonable* level of support.

❝━━━━━━━━━━━━━━ A Comment From the Field ━━━━━━━━━━━━━━

It is extremely stressful to be the mentor to a new teacher who just can't seem to get it together . . . or who doesn't seem to value or even want the support you are trying to provide. Frustration and anxiety build on both sides. Having a team of mentors to advise and support you is so important. Rather than having to go it alone, you have supportive colleagues offering suggestions that you hadn't even considered.

While most of the situations are taken care of with the team's support, I have been through a relationship that, after an extended period of time, just wasn't going to get better. Good suggestions were given, but no signs of action from the new teacher were evident. We determined that it was time for the administrator to become more actively involved in the process.

As a mentor, it took me a while to realize that my mentoring was not a failure, but actually a process that worked to help the new teacher realize what is expected of a teacher.

MCT Member and Experienced Mentor

━━❞

13

How to Identify and Address the Professional Development Needs of Mentors

Our self-report preassessment, **Determining Mentors' and MCT Members' Needs: Self-Assessment** (below), provides MCT members with a way to gather information about the perceived professional strengths and growth needs of their mentors.

The preassessment responses on the following survey should be tabulated in terms of mentor strengths and needs. Use this data to determine the "Mentor Curriculum" that can be "delivered" using a variety of professional development approaches (see **Mentor Professional Development Topics and Recommendations: Guidelines,** below). We suggest using the preassessment each year and then "pacing" the development of your program to meet the specific needs of mentoring teachers in your school. Remember, you can't do everything at once—grow and strengthen your program and your people each year.

> 66 ——— **A Comment From the Field** ———
>
> Being expected to do something you have no idea about . . . is a source of high stress and anxiety! Mentors are high-performing individuals who strive to "be perfect" at everything they do. We have found that giving them the information and allowing them to develop the skills they feel they need to mentor effectively has worked very well for us.
>
> *Experienced Lead Mentor*
> ——————————————— 99

✓ **Research to Practice Insight:** Analysis of preassessments from numerous mentors-in-training reveals that they perceive some mentor roles as much easier to fulfill than others.

Most new mentors generally feel comfortable with their roles as liaison, facilitator, relationship builder, and supporter. Most mentors are nurturers and have confidence in their ability to develop supportive relationships; provide nonjudgmental listening and encouragement; share information about the school and the district; and socialize their protégé into the culture of the school community.

Many new mentors are generally less confident about being a professional role model and often inexperienced in being a coach. They seem to relate less easily to being known as a role model. The main reason may be that they have not had opportunities to develop confidence in their unique strengths. Frequently, we hear very experienced teachers share how they structure their classroom or teach a lesson or unit, but they are not really sure that their actions are "research-based" or considered effective. Likewise, being an effective coach is daunting to many mentors because they have not had opportunities to know what good coaching is or how to do it. Traditional practices of merely assigning a mentor to a new teacher have allowed these insecurities to become accepted practice. We believe that schools and school systems must provide mentors with the knowledge, skills, resources, and time to carry out their responsibilities effectively. First, however, we need to identify their needs, just as we do those of beginning teachers.

DETERMINING MENTORS' AND MCT MEMBERS' NEEDS: SELF-ASSESSMENT

Purpose: To gain specific information about the needs of the educators involved as mentors and/or MCT members in order to plan to provide needed assistance and professional development.

Timing: Prior to or at the beginning of the year

Most new teachers indicate a desire for support in many of the following areas. In order to provide appropriate mentoring, the Mentor Core Team needs to know in what areas you feel most confident and least confident. Our mentor professional development focus for the year will be on addressing the areas you identify as "high need" or "very high need." We have also asked the new teachers to rank each of the items in order to plan our program for the year, using Table 13.1.

Table 13.1 Level of Need

	Little or No Need	Some Need	High Need	Very High Need
Expectations:				
1. for me as a mentor				
2. for me as a member of the MCT				
3. for new teachers' school and system roles and responsibilities				
4. for local and/or state curriculum				
5. of the INTASC standards for beginning teachers (or district/state adopted standards for professional teachers)				
6. of the formal evaluation process for new teachers				
Knowledge of:				
7. the needs of beginning teachers				
8. the school's organizational structure, culture, policies, and procedures				
9. resources available to enhance learning				
10. the cultural norms of our students, families, and school community				
11. the change process and our school improvement priorities				
12. school and school system information, resources, and professional development opportunities available				
13. the mentor process and quality practices				
14. issues related to teacher quality, teacher retention, and varied possibilities for school-based support for new teachers				
15. how to serve as a model of "best practices"				

(Continued)

Table 13.1   (Continued)

	Little or No Need	Some Need	High Need	Very High Need
16. the strengths, talents, and interests of my colleagues that could be shared with new teachers				
17. resources to facilitate professional growth and the development of learning communities				
18. how to coteach with the beginning teacher (if applicable.				
19. collaborative strategies and effective teamwork				
Techniques for helping new teachers:				
20. develop a thorough, in-depth knowledge of the content to be taught				
21. use effective planning strategies to differentiate instruction				
22. use research-based instructional strategies				
23. incorporate varied assessment strategies				
24. design effective classroom management strategies				
25. identify diverse needs of students to use in developing culturally relevant teaching strategies				
26. develop appropriate interpersonal relationships with families, students, and community members				
27. use data to determine the impact of instruction on student learning and to plan future instruction				
28. diagnose student needs and solve problems				
29. develop the ability to self-assess professional skills related to standards and develop plans for future growth				
30. balance personal and professional responsibilities				
Mentoring strategies:				
31. to provide nonjudgmental listening, emotional support, and socialization and/or networking opportunities				
32. to conduct observations (collecting adequate, accurate observation data) and share information with the new teacher				
33. to facilitate meaningful professional growth of colleagues focused on effective teaching and learning				
34. to provide short- and long-term solutions when new teachers encounter obstacles, challenges, or problems				
35. to promote appropriate professional relationships with colleagues				
36. to use mentoring to enhance our Professional Learning Community (learning with and from each other)				
37. to assess the impact of mentoring on new teacher retention and impact on student learning (schoolwide or individually)				

Copyright © 2009 by Corwin Press. All rights reserved. Reprinted from *Mentoring as Collaboration:Lessons From the Field for Classroom, School, and District Leaders* by Mary Ann Blank and Cheryl A. Kershaw. Thousand Oaks, CA: Corwin Press, www.corwinpress.com. Reproduction authorized only for the local school site or nonprofit organization that has purchased this book.

MENTOR PROFESSIONAL DEVELOPMENT TOPICS AND RECOMMENDATIONS: GUIDELINES

Purpose: To develop a mentor curriculum based on needs identified in the Needs Assessment for Mentors and MCT Members

Timing: Initial training or professional development as mentors

Our experience in providing professional development for mentors has reinforced our observations that, in general, even the most skilled and experienced teachers (of children) need and appreciate professional development to fully embrace and implement their roles as mentors. Because most mentors are highly conscientious individuals, they want to mentor effectively. Many find that guiding the learning of children is a far different activity from guiding the learning of adults. As challenging as teaching is, mentoring comes with its own set of "issues." When mentoring moves from informal pairings with general nurturing as the major focus to more substantive relationships with coaching for instructional effectiveness as the goal, we have found that mentors who experience effective (initial and ongoing) professional development (see Table 13.2) related to teacher induction have a much clearer understanding of how to meet the varied needs of new teachers. They gain perspective, become more knowledgeable about research-based strategies, and develop confidence in using the higher-level skills needed to coach adult learners. The results then benefit all—the satisfied new teachers, the rejuvenated mentoring teachers, the proud administrators who see steady progress on improvement priorities, and, most of all, the eager and cooperative students of the new teachers.

> 66 ——— **Comments From the Field** ———
>
> Prior to professional development in being a mentor, we did our best, but we experienced a great deal of frustration because we had no clear idea about expectations for us or [about] specifically what an effective mentor does.
>
> *Fourth-Grade Mentor*
>
> How long does it take to learn to teach? Excellent teachers would say, "Forever!" They know that learning to teach is a complex, long-term, never-ending process. To be able to help new teachers continue on their journey of learning to teach, we have developed an extensive "Mentor Curriculum." We have identified the knowledge and skills mentors must acquire through individual and collective professional learning experiences.
>
> *Large Metropolitan District Professional Development Supervisor* 99

✓ **Research to Practice Insight:** Professional development is a "MUST." It may be provided by educators from within the district if there are experienced mentors who are also able facilitators of adult learning. Or, it may be provided by knowledgeable consultants. We suggest initial training be a minimum of three full days. Participants should attend in school teams (e.g., the administrator and the teacher leaders selected to be mentors) in order to create a common understanding that is translated into school-based action plans. We have found that delivering Days 1 and 2 consecutively during summer is ideal, with Day 3 occurring after several months. This allows MCTs to begin their programs and offers opportunities to share successes and to troubleshoot the challenges. The sessions should meet the mentors' informational and skill needs and be highly interactive with a lot of sharing.

Table 13.2   Initial Professional Development for MCT and Mentors

Possible Topics: Identify your specific topics from the mentor and MCT needs assessment data.

• **Program Goals and Structure**
  o Data and research about the need for mentor program
  o MCT procedures and guidelines
  o Connection to school improvement priorities
  o Link to other school leadership teams/coordination of external mentors
  o School-based support structure (Expert Teams) to support new teachers

• **Expectations**
  o Roles and responsibilities for mentors, lead mentor, MCT members, administrator(s), and new teachers
  o INTASC (or district/state) standards for beginning teachers
  o Mentor yearly plan/checklist of activities
  o Finding time to mentor

• **Informational Needs**
  o Teacher quality, teacher retention, and impact on student learning
  o Typical new teacher needs
  o School-based adjustments to scaffold the transition to teaching (e.g., student assignments, numbers of preparations, adequacy of room and resources, etc.)
  o Commitment to mentoring
  o Accountability procedures

• **Mentor Skills and Strategies**
  o (Beginning Strategies) To meet new teachers' social, emotional, and professional needs
    - Establishing trust, listening actively and empathetically, problem understanding and problem solving
    - [To be determined]
  o (Beginning Skills) To coach new teachers for instructional effectiveness
    - Preparing new teachers for teacher evaluation process
    - [To be determined]

Identify Dates and Plan Activities • **Before the opening of school** • **First Weeks of School** • **First Semester** • **Opening of Second Semester** • **Second Semester** • **Closing of School** • **Summer Break**

14

How to Identify and Address New Teacher Needs

I n 1969, Francis Fuller provided insight into the typical developmental stages through which most new teachers progress.

- **The first stage is self-adequacy—*Will I be able to survive as a teacher?*** New teachers want the students to like and respond positively to them. They want to be accepted and respected by other teachers. They especially want to get favorable evaluations from the principal and other supervisors. Many new teachers are constantly surprised by information they feel they are expected to know, but don't. They quickly become frustrated when they realize that many of their students come to school with many challenges beyond their control, and many struggle with self-efficacy as they lose their confidence in their ability to make a difference in the lives of their students. The most fragile are imbued with feelings of self-doubt and insecurity.

- **The next stage relates to teaching tasks—*Will I be able to actually teach these students given the demanding workload and the inflexible teaching environment?*** New teachers in this stage are experiencing the full and intense pressure associated with their many and varied professional responsibilities. Many feel overwhelmed and alone as they develop teaching routines and deal with discipline and control issues.

66 ——— A Comment From the Field ———

I try to be aware of "where" my protégé is in terms of his developmental stage. When, after an observation, he asks, "How did I do?" I know that he is still at the stage where he is very focused on himself and his basic survival with the students.

Experienced teachers are more concerned about the students and how they are learning and progressing. They generally ask, "How are my students doing?" When they ask this question, I get a lot of satisfaction from knowing that I've helped them make this important transition.

Experienced Mentor

99

• **The final stage is teaching impact—***Am I able to reach all my students in ways that result in maximum student learning?* New teachers at this stage are squarely focused on academic concerns related to diagnosing and meeting students' individual needs. They want to facilitate students' intellectual development and address their emotional and health related needs as well. Their concerns about meeting the needs of the *whole* child lead to related professional development concerns.

Most entry-level teachers are probably at the self-adequacy stage. Mentors should not, however, rule out the possibility of a beginner reaching the "teaching tasks" stage or even the "teaching impact" stage during the first year of teaching. At the same time, mentors should not expect new teachers to be at their same developmental stage. This is often an obstacle that new mentors must overcome!

✓ **Research to Practice Insight:** In the professional life span of teachers, few periods of time compare in impact and importance with the first year of teaching. The beginning of a teaching career for some may be charged with excitement, challenge, and exhilarating success. For others, the first year of teaching may seem to be confusing, uncontrollable, filled with unsolvable problems, and threatened by personal defeat and failure. For many, beginning to teach is a unique and more balanced mixture of success, problems, surprises, and satisfactions. —Johnston & Ryan, 1980

MCTs should use the **Determining New Teachers' Needs: Self-Assessment,** a self-report questionnaire, to gather important information about what new teachers identify as their professional strengths and growth needs. The Lead Mentor, in collaboration with the MCT, can then identify the areas of *collective needs* to plan professional development sessions and *individual needs* to guide in developing an **individualized induction plan** (see **Individualized Induction Plan: Sample Form**, below) for each new teacher and for planning schoolwide professional development opportunities.

We have found that most teacher evaluation processes include a professional growth plan for teachers. Although they are required and revised on an annual basis, many new teachers say that it does not provide specific guidance in focusing their learning, and many feel the plans include so many priorities that they are overwhelming. Many often feel inadequate and unsuccessful because they are attempting to accomplish all expectations at once.

Individual learning plans for each new teacher provide a clearly defined roadmap, but with flexibility to accommodate variations in needs, pacing, and support. Our experience has shown that first-year needs (Level 1) differ significantly from those of second- (Level 2) and third- (Level 3) year teachers. Tailoring these

❝——— A Comment From the Field ———

I think our new teachers reflect the national picture. Most of them are younger are in their early 20s. They are single, in debt or struggling financially. Our other rapidly increasing group is job-changers coming to us through alternative teacher preparation routes. Most of them have content knowledge (gained through degrees or through experience), but [have] limited or no experience with teaching. Many of them struggle with communicating their knowledge to students. Many lack skill in managing and motivating students and have a limited range [of] effective instructional strategies. As we know, it is critical to have all the knowledge about biology, but equally important to be able to motivate students who may not want to learn it!

When these teachers are hired in small, rural high schools, they generally don't have access to mentors with content expertise. So our MCT works hard to "connect" the new teacher with a discipline-alike mentor in a neighboring school that is sometimes in a close-by school system.

Supervisor of Instruction in a Rural School District ❞

plans to the actual needs of new teachers also takes into consideration that some new teachers progress more rapidly than others and each may enter the profession with different strengths.

The example of an individualized induction plan identifies professional growth goals and activities that are linked to the INTASC Standards to help new teachers understand the rationale and focus of the activities. Additional benefits include providing clarity on areas of growth, identifying potential areas of needed assistance, opening lines of communication, and supporting new teachers at each new and unfamiliar stage of development.

✔ **Research to Practice Insight:** Help new teachers expand the scope of professional concerns beyond their own classrooms. Provide opportunities for participation in schoolwide activities that support school improvement, especially those that are of personal interest and within their areas of expertise. Set the expectation that new teachers should contribute to making the classroom and school learning environments as conducive to learning as possible. Be sure new teachers receive the needed professional development to fulfill the expectations. Discuss available PD opportunities.

" A Comment From the Field

We like the idea of a progressive Induction Plan. It keeps the new teachers clearly focused on important priorities for their growth but also for our schoolwide progress on improvement priorities. We have seen that the plans help make the first years successful and somewhat less stressful for our new teachers—and, most important, for their students.

Lead Mentor of a High School MCT

"

DETERMINING NEW TEACHERS' NEEDS: SELF-ASSESSMENT

Purpose: To gain specific information about the needs of the new teachers in order to plan for needed assistance and professional development.

Timing: Prior to or at the beginning of the year

Years of Experience	
_____ 1	_____ None (Preservice teacher)
_____ 2	_____ 4+ (New to the school, not the profession)
_____ 3	

Most new teachers indicate a desire for support in many of the following areas. In order to provide your mentor and our MCT with as much information as possible, please rank each item to reflect your level of need. (Your perceptions or needs may change throughout the year. This is a preassessment (see Table 14.1) that serves as a starting point in working effectively with your mentor.)

Table 14.1   Level of Need

	Little or No Need	*Some Need*	*High Need*	*Very High Need*
Expectations:				
1. for my professional performance				
2. for school and system roles and responsibilities				
3. for local and/or state curriculum to be taught				
4. of the teacher evaluation process				
Knowledge of:				
5. the school's organizational structure, culture, policies, and procedures				
6. the school and school improvement priorities				
7. the school system				
8. the school community				
9. subject areas assigned to teach				
10. effective planning strategies to differentiate instruction				
11. research-based instructional strategies				
12. varied assessment strategies				
13. how to identify and address the diverse needs of my students				
14. how to work effectively with the families of my students				
15. effective classroom management strategies				

	Little or No Need	Some Need	High Need	Very High Need
16. how to balance my personal and professional responsibilities				
Opportunities to:				
17. observe colleagues and discuss teaching and learnings				
18. ask for and receive assistance when challenges or problems are encountered				
19. develop professional relationships with colleagues				
20. develop collaborative skills to learn with and from others				

Please share your honest perceptions with us about the following questions.

1. What do you feel most confident about as you begin your teaching career at this school?

2. What do you anticipate will be your greatest needs during the first few months of the school year?

3. What do you feel you can gain from having a mentor during your induction into the profession and into the culture of this school?

4. What has been most confusing to you during the opening days/weeks of the school year? How can the Mentoring Core Team best address points of confusion?

(Continued)

5. Which types of support do you think would be most helpful to you? Mark all that apply.

_____ One-on-one mentoring

_____ Informal sessions (e.g., before school, during lunch, after school, "Brown Bag Chats")

_____ Periodic workshops at the school on timely issues (e.g., classroom mgt., working with parents, "hands on" learning experiences)

_____ Opportunities to learn from colleagues at the school site

_____ Department meetings

_____ Study groups at the school on topics of common interest

_____ Informal faculty "get togethers"

_____ Systemwide workshops

_____ Access to research (e.g., articles, studies, Web sites)

_____ Other (please explain)

Copyright © 2009 by Corwin Press. All rights reserved. Reprinted from *Mentoring as Collaboration: Lessons From the Field for Classroom, School, and District Leaders* by Mary Ann Blank and Cheryl A. Kershaw. Thousand Oaks, CA: Corwin Press, www.corwinpress.com. Reproduction authorized only for the local school site or nonprofit organization that has purchased this book.

INDIVIDUALIZED INDUCTION PLAN: SAMPLE FORM

Purpose: To provide a "phased in" induction to teaching and to guide a new teacher in accomplishing growth expectations; to identify specific professional development activities linked to INTASC Standards

Timing: At the beginning of the mentoring experience, to be developed with input from the new teacher's self-assessment

SAMPLE Induction Plan for _____.

Level I Expectations

Basic priorities that should be required for new teachers	*INTASC PRINCIPLE(S)*
Accomplish long- and short-range curriculum pacing	#7: Planning Instruction
Develop monthly substitute teacher lesson plan	#7: Planning Instruction
Analyze student grades and test scores—with mentor(s)	#8: Assessment
Design effective Instructional Units and Lessons—Incorporate strategies to address diverse learners and meet IEPs	#7: Planning Instruction #4: Instructional Strategies
Develop classroom management plan	#5: Learning Environment
Strengthen knowledge of content and curriculum expectations	#1: Subject Matter #2: Student Learning
Make introductory calls to parents/guardians of students	#6: Communication
Engage in extracurricular activities that are short-term, with limited time commitment and responsibility	#10: Collaboration, Ethics, and Relationships
Understand and follow legal and recordkeeping requirements	#10: Collaboration, Ethics, and Relationships
Needed Resources and Strategies: [To Be Identified]	

Level II Expectations

Next-level priorities that should be required for most new teachers	*INTASC PRINCIPLE(S)*
Accomplish long- and short-range curriculum pacing—collaboratively and independently	#7: Planning Instruction
Continue to strengthen knowledge of content and curriculum expectations	#1: Subject Matter #2: Student Learning
Refine units and lessons to incorporate differentiated strategies	#3: Diverse Learners #4: Instructional Strategies
Analyze student grades and test scores—verified by mentor(s)	#8: Assessment
Develop differentiated assessment strategies (pre-, during, and post-)	#8: Assessment #1: Subject Matter #2: Student Learning #3: Diverse Learners

(Continued)

Level II Expectations (Continued)

Next-level priorities that should be required for most new teachers	INTASC PRINCIPLE(S)
Engage in extracurricular activities that are short-term, with limited time commitment and responsibility	#10: Collaboration, Ethics, and Relationships
Implement family communications strategy (e.g., Class Web site or Weekly Newsletters, other)	#6: Communication
Needed Resources and Strategies: [To Be Identified]	

Level III Expectations

The highest-level priorities that should be required for most novice teachers	INTASC PRINCIPLE(S)
Continue to strengthen knowledge of content and curriculum expectations	#1: Subject Matter #2: Student Learning
Analyze student grades and test scores (independently), refine assessment strategies (pre-, during, and post-), and develop plans that incorporate additional differentiated strategies	#8: Assessment #7: Planning Instruction #3: Diverse Learners #4: Instructional Strategies
Collaborate with mentor to develop differentiated, meaningful-use projects (or alternative assessments) with rubric(s); study the effects of projects using action research model of professional inquiry	#8: Assessment #7: Planning Instruction #3: Diverse Learners #4: Instructional Strategies #9: Reflection and Professional Development
Continue family communications strategy	#6: Communication
Assume expanded leadership in school improvement or extracurricular activities, as time/work load permits	#10: Collaboration, Ethics, and Relationships
Needed Resources and Strategies: [To Be Identified]	

Copyright © 2009 by Corwin Press. All rights reserved. Reprinted from *Mentoring as Collaboration: Lessons From the Field for Classroom, School, and District Leaders* by Mary Ann Blank and Cheryl A. Kershaw. Thousand Oaks, CA: Corwin Press, www.corwinpress.com. Reproduction authorized only for the local school site or nonprofit organization that has purchased this book.

15

How to Meet New Teachers' Social, Emotional, and Professional Needs

Mentoring Strategies

Constructive and supportive one-on-one relationships between mentors and new teachers are built on trust. To effectively provide the social-emotional support most new teachers need, trust is critical—and must be earned and maintained. Trust between a mentor and a protégé is tested on a daily basis by each individual's actions and interactions. School-related interpersonal relationships must begin with positive assumptions and are strengthened through supportive actions. We have seen that in schools where there are numerous positive, professional role models and distributed support among faculty and staff, new teachers grow steadily into strong teachers and leaders.

Building relationships also involves purposeful activities designed to build new teachers' confidence and competence. Just as it is with students and their first days of school, so it is with new teachers. Those first introductions to colleagues and encounters with the new school environment set the tone for the days and weeks that follow.

> ## 66 —— A Comment From the Field ——
>
> Trust can be elusive. As mentors, we must "walk the talk" every day with our protégés. We say, "Come to me at anytime with any question." Then, when they do come, we must put our own needs on hold and respond with concern and patience. Also, as mentors we must develop short-term mentoring strategies to effectively meet new teachers' emergency situations, but also to use longer-term, preventive strategies to avoid the reactive approach required during times of crisis.
>
> *High School Lead Mentor*
> 99

New teachers need to know about the important external influences on their teaching (i.e., SIP, NCLB, discipline policies, state rules and regulations, any grants or special initiatives, etc., as shown in **External Influences: Guidelines**, below). To assist in their development as effective instructors, MCTs assure that they gain an understanding of the organizational structure of the school, its culture and governance, the school community, and the multiple resources available to them. With this information in hand, new teachers can more easily incorporate familiar, contextual elements into instruction and connect with parents and families in ways that will enhance their students' learning.

We have seen that much of mentoring for schoolwide social-emotional support and informational needs can be accomplished by the MCT. Included in the **Annual Mentoring Activities: Checklist** presented in Chapter 12 are activities facilitated by the team to benefit all new teachers. Welcome Baskets, a New Teacher Shower, Beginning of School Luncheon, and a New Teacher Network are some of the activities that are planned and hosted by the team to introduce the new teachers to the faculty and promote relationship-building. Community Mapping (see **School Community: Guidelines,** below; Treadway, 2000) is a process designed to help teachers at any experience level better understand the school's community—the assets, challenges, and resources. Need-to-know information is presented through "Brown Bag Chats" (informational sessions focused on one topic, held during lunch time) or 30-Minute Thursdays (brief professional development sessions facilitated by mentors on timely, specific topics scheduled throughout the year), in a New Teacher Handbook developed and updated by the MCT, or by designated faculty on the school's Expert Teams. Even when the district provides an initial orientation, many of the new teachers' "unasked" questions can be answered in a safer environment in more productive and specific ways (see **School Faculty and Policy: Guidelines,** below). Completed sample forms specific to the school are usually included as helpful models. To acquaint new teachers with the organization of the school, some schools use a Scavenger Hunt to help them locate people and supplies; complete required forms, such as accounting, absence, professional leave; and meet staff members. Other schools encourage new teachers to shadow counselors and principals for a few hours to better understand why school policies are in place and the consequences when teachers and/or students do not follow them.

SCHOOL COMMUNITY: GUIDELINES

- Arrange for a new teacher tour of the community and school zone or the entire feeder area.
- Orient new teachers to the cultures represented by the student body, the staff, and the community.
- Arrange for new teachers to meet representatives of the various cultures represented.
- Invite parenting adults and appropriate others to share information about their culture and customs.
- Begin or update written information, Web sites, or videos about the cultures represented—*need-to-know information*—including helpful instructional suggestions.
- Share a calendar of community events and sites of interest.
- Identify potential community mentors who would be willing to collaborate with new teachers.
- Begin a digital resource file of pictures of the community to incorporate in lessons.
- Develop a list of resources and contact information for community agencies, service providers, adopters, and so on. Visit and talk with these representatives, if possible.

✓ **Research to Practice Insight:** Use Community Mapping as a strategy to connect beginning teachers to their new school community.

First developed by Treadway in 2000 for the Contextual Teaching and Learning Project with support from The Ohio State University and the U.S. Department of Education, community mapping is a process for systematically gathering information about a community that focuses on identifying assets as well as challenges. It also breaks down teachers' stereotypes about communities that differ significantly from their own. As teachers engage in community mapping, they talk with parents and community members. They come to realize that all parents really do care, but many do not seem to know how to access resources available to them.

Every school community has both a historical record and current resources that can enhance teaching and learning. Until school personnel actively explore their communities, they miss the opportunity to incorporate students' everyday experience into their instruction in ways that make learning experiences more relevant to students' lives. The relationship between a community and a school should be a two-way street. Both have something to offer, but making that a reality requires that teachers know both what is available and how to make use of that knowledge in designing culturally and contextually relevant instruction. How can educators make learning relevant to the lives of students if they do not understand what these lives entail? How can they build upon the strengths that students and their families bring to the learning process without talking with them and learning about their unique backgrounds and characteristics?

MENTORING STRATEGIES

SCHOOL FACULTY AND POLICY: GUIDELINES

- Organize a schoolwide scavenger hunt for the new teachers. Include need-to-know people (give advance warning!), places, and equipment.
- Send new teachers on a "Beg-Borrow-Steal" adventure during which new teachers could acquire helpful ideas or resources by begging, borrowing, and "stealing."

Figure 15.1   New Teacher Shower Ideas

Ready-to-go bulletin boards for upcoming months
Sample "sponge" activities to fill in unexpected minutes
Educational games that you know the students like
Favorite Web sites for student enrichment activities
Sample novel study (or any other type) units
Sample newsletters (paper and electronic forms)

- Surprise new teachers with a Care Package or Welcome Basket. Include important teacher items such as colored chalk/pens, sticky notes, fall bulletin board materials, get-acquainted activities to do with students, tissue, and copy codes. A set of stamped post cards would be good to start on teacher-home communications.
- Provide a school calendar. Point out significant dates, and talk about how to be prepared for those dates. The days before and after holidays, picture days, and annual distribution days tend to be times when continuity of instruction is challenging.
- Provide information about central office personnel, their responsibilities, and contact information. Perhaps arranging an introduction would be helpful.
- Give an annual facebook, if available, so new teachers can become acquainted with some faces. Also provide contact numbers and e-mail addresses for faculty and staff.
- Provide (or develop) (New) Teacher Guide including policies, procedures for money collection, hall passes, tardies, discipline referrals, field trips, homework, special education referrals, guidelines for M- and S-team meetings.
- Ask teachers to supply their best strategies for saving time—working smarter, not harder. (Could be included in the New Teacher Shower or Care Package.)

SCHOOL CULTURE: GUIDELINES

✓ **Research to Practice Insight:** Researchers report impressive evidence on the effects of collaborative school cultures marked by high expectations and collegial support. According to Richard Sagor (2003), research has increasingly shown that the professional culture of the organization is the single best predictor of increased student success. Specifically, healthy school cultures correlate strongly with increased student achievement and motivation, and with teacher productivity and satisfaction.

- Focus on the importance of collaboration, and orient new teachers to teamwork expectations. Help them understand the expected (and productive) behaviors of team members. Work with them to know how to be a contributing member of a team.
- Ask colleagues to invite new teachers to accompany them to extracurricular activities. This would be a good way for new teachers to see the range of activities and identify those they would like to be involved in (at some future time). They could also invite new teachers to attend meetings or events sponsored by professional organizations.
- Organize a new teacher support group—face to face or electronic. Only new teachers allowed!
- Offer to be an "editor" to any communications to be sent home or posted. Also, provide practice or role-play what is expected in M- and S-team meetings, parent conferences, and open houses. The goal is to help new teachers develop their confidence and their ability to communicate effectively. Developing sensitivity to communication styles and language helps new teachers gain the respect and acceptance of students, parents, and colleagues.

" ━━━━━━━━━━ **Comments From the Field** ━━━━━━━━━━

Our motto has become "Set new teachers up for success, not failure." We are finding ways to overcome the traditional barriers to new teacher success—the toughest work assignments, including numbers of preparations or challenging students, and time-consuming extracurricular obligations; unclear expectations; isolation; lack of emotional support; inadequate resources, materials, and information. It requires making some difficult decisions and challenges some long-held traditions related to seniority, but in the end, everyone benefits.

Mentor Core Team Chair

Our New Teacher Handbook was created as a team effort by members of the MCT. Their goal was to be PREVENTIVE—to communicate need-to-know information consistently to all new teachers, especially those who are hired as long-term subs or at points other than the beginning of the year. They felt it was important to not leave communication of information left unsaid or to chance; they put it in writing. Expectations are presented with opportunities to discuss and clarify. Now, all we do is update and revise it as needed.

High School Principal

"

MENTORING STRATEGIES

Figure 15.2 New Teacher Handbook Table of Contents (Sample)

Teacher Job Description
Advice about performing professional responsibilities efficiently and effectively

Board Policies and Regulations
Student Rights Laws
Advice about related teacher responsibilities

School Improvement Plan
Need-to-Know information and related teacher responsibilities

School Professional Learning Communities
(including In-house Expert Teams)

Individualized Induction Plan
Guidelines, Procedures, and Corrective Actions
Current Professional Development Resources

School, System, and Community Events Calendar

School, Community, and System Contact Information
(Who does What)

Teacher Evaluation Process
Dates and Forms (Completed as Samples)

School-Specific Routines and Procedures

New Teacher Commitment to Mentor

Survival Tips
(Advice about the power of collaboration and being a team player; Dos and Don'ts in establishing respectful and productive relationships with parents and guardians, community or parent volunteers, colleagues, mentors, and students, etc.)

66 ———————————— **Comments From the Field** ————————————

Before we had so many new teachers, we really didn't have an extensive professional library. Our MCT decided to create one that includes helpful teacher resources, materials, professional publications, trade samples, etc. We found that having materials in a central location with our standard checkout system made access easier and made better use of the resources. We also created a teacher wish list so teachers could request needed resource books or materials to use for instructional activities, such as recycled materials and items others may have, know about, or could collect.

Librarian Member of an Elementary MCT

When our MCT was compiling information for new teachers for their handbook, we began thinking of all the "unwritten" rules in effect in our school—don't interrupt the principal when she is walking down the hall with her clipboard, chocolate chip cookies are the janitor's favorite, never ask a question of the secretary if she is counting money, etc. We laughed and had a great time, but realized that we couldn't put any of that in writing!

Middle School Mentor

—— 99

EXTERNAL INFLUENCES: GUIDELINES

• Share the School Improvement Plan. Review and discuss in detail to ensure understanding. Be sure that new teachers comprehend the data, underlying reasons for the actions, their responsibilities, and monitoring/accountability procedures. In addition, new teachers need opportunities to learn about the recommended strategies and how to use them. Their knowledge of the targets and the strategies being used is critical to new teachers' commitment to the plan.

• Share information about the Teacher Evaluation and Professional Growth process. Most MCTs provide samples of any required forms completed with appropriate and adequate information to serve as models. Other teams engage in role-plays to model conferences, if any are involved. Focus on the standards, and talk about the ways in which effective teachers exhibit the expected behaviors. One team focused on one standard at a time, and everyone added their ideas about what an exemplary teacher does, says, and acts like related to that standard. They felt the brainstorming activity contributed to everyone's developing a better understanding of the standards.

66 ———— **A Comment From the Field** ————

As an administrator responsible for many evaluations of new teachers, the work the MCT does to orient and coach them about the evaluation process has really made my job of evaluation much easier. The new teachers are much more comfortable with the whole process and, with lessened anxiety, they are able to relax and do their usual excellent job of teaching. I've also seen that the veteran teachers who are mentors have a much better understanding of the standards.

Intermediate School Principal

———————————————————— 99

• Share information about additional influences such as NCLB, grants, school board policies, community expectations, and so on.

16

How to Coach New Teachers for Instructional Effectiveness

Coaching Strategies

The mentor role of **Coach** is perhaps the most significant one in terms of accelerating the new teacher's instructional effectiveness. Again, trust is a critical element in maintaining a relationship that produces growth. We know from the research on effective teaching that providing corrective feedback is a significant teacher behavior. Mentors must also be able to give honest, objective, and constructive feedback about instruction and its effects on learning. When mentors share feedback in this manner, trust is strengthened and growth is promoted. We encounter many mentors, especially new ones, who need professional development and practice in order to address instructional improvement and coach in highly effective ways. After initial professional development on coaching strategies, experienced MCT members can share the techniques they use to promote new teachers' constructive analysis and problem solving, reflection, and action. Mentors can develop their expertise in standards-based coaching and skillfully guide new teachers from dependent novices to independent, fully functioning professionals and teacher leaders.

Mentor Core Teams have recommended the following coaching strategies as highly valued. Many MCTs hold regular development sessions on specific strategies identified by mentors as areas to grow. We also recommend, if resources permit, the capacity building opportunity to engage in Cognitive Coaching training (Costa & Garmston, 1994).

✓ **Research to Practice Insight: The mentor is the coach, NOT an evaluator.** The coach prepares his or her protégé for the formal evaluation process; it is the administrator's responsibility to conduct the process and be the evaluator. It is critical that no actions undermine the trust between the mentor and protégé.

FREQUENT AND ONGOING COMMUNICATION: GUIDELINES

Why? To promote trust, to assess new teacher's level of development and teacher thinking; to notice and acknowledge progress; to identify needed interventions

How To? Be available and accessible; listen empathetically with "understanding" from the new teacher's perspective; listen actively using accepting, clarifying, paraphrasing, questioning, probing, and acknowledging statements; respond with descriptive feedback that accurately describes the situation without being evaluative (which may lead to defensiveness) or interpretive (based on assumptions that may be inaccurate)

66 ——— **A Comment From the Field** ———

One mentor behavior I had to work on was using more "neutral" language when responding to my protégé. My usual responses were more "evaluative," such as "great," "super idea," "very good." I had to work on using language that showed I was listening and accepting what was being shared, such as "I see" or "I can follow your thinking" rather than judging every statement.

Experienced Mentor

99

REFLECTIVE PRACTICE: GUIDELINES

Why? To "pause" the action long enough to gain perspective; to redirect focus on the students and their learning; to attempt to look beyond the result to determine the possible cause (so that it may be avoided—or used more often—in future interactions).

How To? Ask more probing questions that lead to identifying antecedent behaviors or situations that may have led to the result; ask "why do you think that happened?" or "what was going on [at the time of the incident]?" This discussion may reveal constructive approaches. In some schools, beginning teachers are asked to videotape teaching segments two to three times during the year. Afterward, the mentor and new teacher reflect together on the lesson. Taping across time also offers opportunities to acknowledge and celebrate progress. It is motivational for new teachers to see how far they have come!

✓ **Research to Practice Insight:** Coaching is an ongoing process building from one episode to the next. Effective mentors point out specific evidence as a way to recognize and acknowledge professional growth. They also enact a recommended strategy by Feiman-Nemser (2001) which is to model "wondering about teaching." They validate the complexity of many teaching-learning situations by not always having a ready answer! They want to give objective, descriptive information and engage in thoughtful problem solving. Sometimes that requires "time to reflect" from the mentor.

DATA-BASED PROBLEM SOLVING: GUIDELINES

❝── A Comment From the Field ──

Many new teachers are so focused on themselves and their insecurities. As a way to get the point across and have some fun with it, we often use the phrase "Remember, it is not about you!"

Experienced Mentor

❞

Why? To model a process of using evidence or information, not intuition or emotional feelings, to identify possible solutions; or to guide transfer of data-based problem solving to new teachers so that it becomes a "habit."

How To? When observing, create a record that accurately describes the facts; carefully guard against making assumptions about the situation. When conferencing, ask questions to clarify the events, times, people, and surrounding conditions to ascertain the facts. Ask questions such as "What did you see or hear?" and "What didn't you see or hear that you think might be important?"

✓ **Research to Practice Insight:** It is challenging for mentors to give feedback that is evaluative in nature. One suggestion is to express it with some qualification, or in the form of a question, e.g., "I wonder if . . ." or "What do you think about . . . ?" Mentors often need to go beyond just questioning. Mentors become skilled in using questions or comments as an opportunity to arrive at a clear understanding of the situation. They learn to avoid using statements such as "I think you should . . ." or "Here's the way I would have done it." Because they see that descriptions rather than interpretations or evaluations keep the focus on the facts, not assumptions.

—The Consultancy Protocol from the Annenberg Institute for School Reform

"COACHABLE" MOMENTS: GUIDELINES

Why? To seize opportunities as they present themselves; to go with the new teacher's "agenda," questions, or immediate concerns. Put your "mentor agenda" on hold—until the timing is right.

How To? For a coach, a range of important topics must be explored and discussed. If the pacing and timing are, for the most part, determined by the new teacher, more professional learning will take place. Coaches need to be organized in noting topics requiring discussion at later times.

✔ **Research to Practice Insight:** One way to find "coachable" moments is to use some techniques borrowed from Cognitive Coaching (Costa & Garmston, 1994). When your protégé has planned an upcoming lesson, hold a preconference prior to the lesson to debrief the planning. Help new teachers begin to focus on critical elements of effective planning by asking questions. Coaches' questions should focus on being specific in identifying and communicating curriculum objectives, identifying important characteristics of the learners, using a range of effective teaching strategies to differentiate instruction, being able to visualize the sequencing and pacing the lesson, and thinking about the evidence in judging the lesson's success in terms of students' learning, engagement, and motivation.

Mentors who develop skill at asking questions, probing, and restating responses as ways to promote rethinking help their protégés develop more effective plans. They also begin to "get inside the new teacher's heads" and gain key insights into teacher thinking.

An additional benefit is that this opportunity allowed valuable coaching—and, it required only 10 minutes! Even if the mentor does not observe the lesson, he or she has helped the new teacher be more prepared and intentional in teaching it—the "verbal rehearsal" has many benefits. A similar process can be used when guiding the new teacher in reflecting on the lesson after it has been taught.

STRATEGIC SCAFFOLDING: GUIDELINES

Why? To provide the type of assistance and support that is consistent with the new teacher's knowledge and skill levels, and to grow the novice into an independent, fully functioning professional at a rate consistent with his or her needs.

How To? At the beginning of the mentorship with most protégés, mentors need to be more directive in their approach. This is when new teachers have not had the experience and have not yet acquired the knowledge or skills. As the protégé matures, mentors can become more collaborative and nondirective in their approach.

66 —— **A Comment From the Field** ——

I sometimes find that I have to deviate from my focus and save my immediate concerns until a later time. If my protégé is more concerned about a topic we will get to at some future point, why not deal with it now? I've found this leads to satisfaction on all sides!

Experienced Mentor

99

✓ **Research to Practice Insight:** We learned from Gray & Associates (1985) to think of the mentor-protégé relationship as a continuum that ranges from **Mp** (Mentor dominant) at the beginning of the relationship to **MP** (more reciprocal, collaborative) as the protégé gains more knowledge and experience to **mP** (Protégé dominant) when the protégé has grown to the level of being a productive, independent professional—which, for the "health" of the organization, is the level we desire for all educators.

Mp to **MP** to **mP**

We learned from Glickman (1985) that each stage requires a different mentoring approach, with **Mp** requiring a more **Directive** approach, **MP** a more **Collaborative** one, and **mP** a more **Nondirective** approach.

We have learned from many mentors-in-training that the majority prefer to be less directive and more collaborative in their approaches to coaching. What many have learned is that working with new teachers requires the use of all approaches depending on individual characteristics and situational conditions. Many find that some protégés and some situations require a mentor to be more directive. When a protégé is not responding appropriately to a nondirective approach, a coach must move out of his or her "comfort zone" and provide more assertive, straightforward messages. It may not be comfortable, but it is appropriate and will be more effective.

MODELING: GUIDELINES

Why? To help new teachers *visualize* important instructional procedures such as using graphic organizers, cooperative learning, or a decision-making matrix. Seeing a procedure in action is the first step in helping them acquire the process.

How To? Following Marzano's (1997) model for acquiring procedural knowledge in *Dimensions of Learning*, mentors should first help new teachers **Construct a model** for the specific process, then allow practice using the procedure to **Shape the model** to make it their own, and then, with continued use, to **Internalize the model.**

Important Coaching Points With Modeling

- Share the steps of the model or important considerations.
- Present the model using "Think-Aloud" strategy to highlight "teacher thinking." Also, provide your rationale for actions, and emphasize the steps of the process.
- Practice the model to "own it." As new teachers practice using the model, they can make careful adaptations that make the model "work" for them. *Cloning* is not the goal (figure 16.1), but using the model with integrity in ways that are consistent with the teacher's style is. Mentor feedback is especially important at this step.
- The goal is for new teachers to reach *automaticity* in using the teaching strategy or model in various teaching and learning situations and content areas with quality results.

PLANNING COLLABORATIVELY: GUIDELINES

Why? To provide a collegial model and a two-way process that begins with the mentor providing model lessons, units, pacing guides, and plan books. At first, mentors lead the discussion and analysis of key best practices. Planning can then move to a more reciprocal level, with new teachers adding ideas of their own. At some future point, new teachers will have grown to the point where they are providing the models!

How To? Take the lead in sharing your experienced perspective, research, or other professional knowledge as an important way to transfer needed information. Provide research-based models for units of instruction, daily lesson plans, advance organizers for instructional units, and assessment strategies. It may also be helpful to provide resources that will help strengthen new teachers' knowledge of content and skills to be taught.

Figure 16.1   No Cloning

COACHING STRATEGIES

OBSERVING INSTRUCTION: GUIDELINES

Why? To be "another pair of eyes" in the classroom; to gather data about teaching and learning events and interactions; to provide information about important instructional processes of presenting instruction, engaging students in learning opportunities, managing and motivating students, using efficient routines to manage events including transitions, and so on.

How To? Observing instruction is a most significant process for promoting a new teacher's growth in professional practice. It usually is an unfamiliar process for mentors, but one that can be mastered with concentrated and educative practice. Detailed observation guidelines and data collection strategies are found in Resource A. Mentors should give the observation notes to protégés so that trust and confidentiality are maintained.

ANALYZING DATA: GUIDELINES

Why? To examine evidence or results in a thoughtful, professional manner, leading to a better understanding about standards of quality work and acceptable performance levels; to review student assessment results and samples of teacher or student work that can reveal critical issues related to teaching and learning. It is also important to determine the match between curriculum objectives, instruction, and assessment strategies.

> 66 ——— **A Comment From the Field** ———
>
> After reviewing the research on the importance of feedback to students, we talked about how important helpful feedback is to our new teachers. We all used Interactive Journals with our protégés to record information or to respond to questions, and decided that was the perfect way to communicate specific feedback about significant actions we observe on a daily basis. Our school is organized in open-spaced pods. Observing one another's actions occurs throughout every day. Prior to recording the feedback in the journals, it was often left unsaid, not intentionally, but due to our fast-paced lives. The opportunity to pass on important coaching tips just didn't happen. We realized that we had missed excellent opportunities to reinforce and enhance the learning of our new teachers.
>
> *Lead Mentor of an Elementary MCT*
>
> 99

How To? Help the beginning teacher learn how to disaggregate data about his or her students (i.e., by ability level, interests, intelligences). Model the planning of several lessons and then a unit of instruction to incorporate appropriate challenges for students in each ability group. With the new teacher, reflect upon how well students in each group performed against their expected outcomes. There are also numerous structured protocols that could be used to guide data-based reflection. (For more information about collaborative analysis, see Critical Friends Protocols (2001) and Langer, Colton, & Goff (2003).)

CONFERENCING AND MAKING RECOMMENDATIONS: GUIDELINES

Why? To share important information in a collegial conference so that effective, neutral, and ineffective patterns of instruction can be identified. At this point, mentors should use the problem-solving protocol to help the new teacher improve the patterns that are not producing desired student learning results.

How To? Guide the new teacher by focusing on only a few *priority* recommendations as a way to avoid overload. It is helpful to think about the complexity of the recommendations—some are much more challenging to implement than others. It is also constructive to build on positive elements already incorporated in the lesson or plans. Moving from a familiar structure or strategy to something less familiar is an easier transition for new teachers.

GIVING FEEDBACK AND MAKING DATA-BASED INSTRUCTIONAL DECISIONS: GUIDELINES

Why? Providing objective, data-based feedback promotes the growth of students and of teachers. In the case of new teachers, it must be related to professional teaching standards consistent with research-based instructional practice.

How To? A major reference for providing research-based feedback is presented in Resource B. It was created using INTASC (Interstate New Teacher Assessment and Support Consortium), which is the Council of Chief State School Officers' *Model Standards for Beginning Teacher Licensing, Assessment and Development: A Resource for State Dialogue* (1992). Resource B is a listing of possible recommendations based on research and best practices organized by INTASC Principle. It was included due to the positive feedback received from mentors and principals. Many said that they keep it as a ready reference when attempting to identify or to phrase constructive recommendations.

PLANNING ACTION ON RECOMMENDATIONS: GUIDELINES

Why? Some recommendations are more difficult to implement than others, and new teachers often need guidance in seeing how to actually *act on* even fairly simple recommendations. Complex ones may require a great deal of thought and planning.

Effective mentors do not merely tell new teachers to "improve student behavior." Many new teachers would not know how to begin acting on such an encompassing recommendation. Skillful mentors provide guidance in breaking complex tasks down into doable and prioritized steps.

How To? Through collaborative planning, work with the new teacher to incorporate the recommendations in lesson and unit plans. Identify specific times when specific research-based actions or strategies could be included. Offer to serve as a coach or a "second set of eyes" as they are implemented. Guide the new teacher to decisions about the most appropriate strategies.

66 ——————————————— **A Comment From the Field** ———————————

As mentors we are focused on our protégé's response of "everything's going fine." All too often we have accepted that response when we have asked, "How is it going today?" We have realized that typically we don't probe or ask for clarification. We just say "great" and move on to our next important thing to do. We are now very aware that we were missing good opportunities for "teachable moments." It may be due to the pressure we feel and the lack of quality time. We are now trying to be more specific in our communications. We continue to ask the question, but now we realize that we must be ready for the real answer. If something isn't going well, it needs to be addressed. If we are serious about dealing with the tough issues our new teachers are facing, we need to devote time to understand the challenges and to find potential solutions.

Elementary Mentor

—— 99

COACHING STRATEGIES

Part IV

Assessing the Impact of Your Mentor Program

As the old adage states, "What you value, you plan for and monitor." In Parts II and III, we have defined the components of an effective school-based mentoring program and provided guidelines and plans for designing and implementing your program. The key to assuring a quality program is systematically assessing its impact on all stakeholders—new teachers, mentors, and, most important, students. Unfortunately, this essential component is often minimally addressed, if at all.

Both research and practice concur that effective mentoring is professional development at its highest level. According to Killion (2003) and Guskey (2002), mentor programs should be assessed on criteria for quality professional development with impact on student achievement as its highest level. The recommendations in this chapter are aligned with these criteria and Guskey's (2002) multitiered model for determining the impact of professional development below. His levels of impact, which range from lowest impact (Level 1) to highest impact (Level 5), are as follows:

Guskey's Model for Determining the Impact of Professional Development

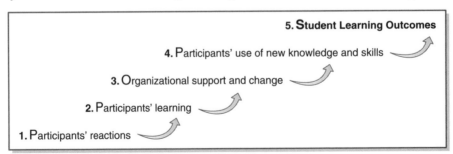

5. **Student Learning Outcomes**

4. Participants' use of new knowledge and skills

3. Organizational support and change

2. Participants' learning

1. Participants' reactions

Guskey's model provides guidance for planning and reflection, particularly if Mentor Core Teams follow his advice to plan with the end in mind. This means starting with the impact of all mentoring activities on student learning and working backward. Ask hard questions such as "How are new teacher assignments (challenging courses, multiple planning requirements) or working conditions (sharing classrooms, most challenging students) impacting their ability to help their students learn?" If school or systemwide leadership teams answer questions like these honestly, it will end the "sink-or-swim" approach to inducting new teachers into our profession.

This Part provides a variety of strategies designed to assess the impact of your program to facilitate its growth, improvement, and the celebration of successes (see below). Many of the data sources are already part of your school improvement planning process. Other data sources and assessment instruments have not traditionally been used by schools to evaluate the effectiveness of mentoring practices. Traditional assessments of mentoring have focused on tracking the numbers of teachers who leave teaching or traditional schools, not the reasons why they leave or choose to stay. If assessing your program is viewed as an integral part of its development, and addressing obstacles and celebrating successes is part of your school culture, you are on the way to developing a real learning community.

Assessing Your School's Mentor Program

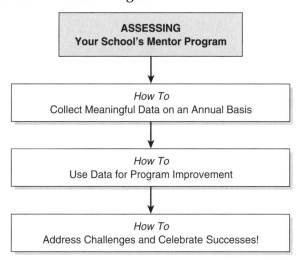

" ─────────────── A Comment From the Field ───────────────

I am absolutely amazed at what is happening with our school-based mentoring program. From the data we are now collecting, we know that we have drastically cut our attrition rate in most of our highest-need schools and better understand teacher perceptions of their first years of teaching and the mentoring they were provided. Most of our 80 Mentor Core Teams have been instrumental in promoting collaboration in their buildings, and many are contributing to our system's commitment to building site-based learning communities. These teacher leadership teams are using data to drive how they work together to assure that students are the focus of all of their mentoring and professional development efforts. Some are "fine-tuning" well-organized programs. Others are at a far more basic stage—and that's OK. They are working together to grow their program and tailor it to their own unique context. Assessing the program and documenting impact, at both the school and system level, is the key to our being able to identify these trends and support the schools at the system level. Even with room to grow, we now have something in place that most systems just dream about.

Supervisor of Professional Development

"

17

How to Collect Meaningful Data on an Annual Basis

Effective mentoring teams systematically collect and analyze data from a variety of sources throughout the year to assess their impact and progress toward clearly defined goals. Formative data are used to make mid-course programmatic changes to address unanticipated conditions, problems, or outcomes. Summative data, generally gathered at the end of each school year, indicate whether or not the program is achieving its intended outcomes and are often used to make decisions about whether or not a program is to be continued and how it should be revised. Both formative and summative data sources are readily available to school-based Mentor Core Teams and to school districts.

The following framework (Table 17.1), adapted from Guskey's (2002) Levels of Professional Development, provides reflective questions, suggestions for data collection (formative and summative), and use of the data collected regarding the five levels of impact of the mentoring program.

Table 17.1 Guiding Questions for Reflection and Evaluation

Levels	Guiding Questions for Reflection and Evaluation	Possible Data Sources	Use of Data
Level 1: Participants' Reactions (Mentors' and new teachers' reactions to their professional development)	• Do participants perceive their professional development to adequately prepare them for their roles and responsibilities? • Do mentors feel that they have been provided with all the necessary tools to become an effective mentor? • Are materials considered appropriate and helpful? • Are presenters knowledgeable and prepared? • Are professional development sessions held at appropriate times and in comfortable settings?	• Questionnaires at the end of professional development sessions • Questionnaires or surveys (end of each semester) • Focus group interviews	Program Improvement: design and delivery
Level 2: Participants' Learning (Mentors' and new teachers' perceptions of their learning from the professional development)	• Did participants acquire the intended knowledge and skills? • Did the learning experience impact participants' beliefs and professional practices? • Do new teachers perceive their mentoring support to be positively impacting their professional growth? • Do mentors perceive their professional development to have impacted their own professional practice and their ability to help new teachers? • Are the mentor/new teacher pairings perceived as facilitating learning of the new teachers and coaching by mentors? • Does the program structure promote the learning of new teachers and mentors?	• MCT Implementation and Impact Rubric • Participant reflections (e.g., surveys, questionnaires of new teachers and mentors) • Focus group interviews • Teacher evaluations • New teacher portfolios or evaluation data • Mentor Needs Assessment	Program Improvement: identification and articulation of professional growth, outcomes, content, format, and organization
Level 3: Organizational Support and Change (Mentor Program)	• Is support public and overt? • Are problems addressed quickly and resolved efficiently and constructively? • Are resources (time, money, space, scheduling) adequate and available? • Are successes recognized and shared? • Is the program producing continuous improvement in the school as an organization, school climate, policies, and mentoring structure?	• Mentor Core Team Implementation and Impact Rubric • Participant reflections (e.g., surveys, questionnaires, focus groups) • Meeting minutes • Teacher retention data • School and Classroom Climate Assessments	Program Improvement: organizational support, policies, and procedures

(Continued)

DATA COLLECTION

DATA COLLECTION

Table 17.1   (Continued)

Levels	Guiding Questions for Reflection and Evaluation	Possible Data Sources	Use of Data
Level 4: Participants' Use of New Knowledge and Skills (Mentors' and new teachers' transfer of their learning from the professional development sessions)	• Are new teachers and mentors able to effectively apply the knowledge and skills gained through professional development in their classrooms (e.g., establishing a positive classroom climate, lesson planning, differentiated instruction, incorporating varied assessment strategies, working with parents, the evaluation process)? • Are mentors able to demonstrate the ability to support and coach new teachers effectively? • Are new teachers using professional development learning in their professional roles?	• Mentor Core Team Implementation and Impact Rubric • Participant reflections (surveys, questionnaires, or interviews) • Focus groups • Meeting minutes • Observation data • Videos or audio tapes (mentoring instruction) • Mentor/MCT Record of Activities	Program Improvement: degree and quality of program implementation, coaching, mentoring support, and progress toward program goals
Level 5: Student Learning Outcomes (In mentors' and new teachers' classrooms)	• Did the professional development result in desired student learning outcomes? 1. academic achievement (grades, test scores) 2. classroom performance (observation, anecdotal records) 3. physical or emotional well-being 4. motivation to learn 5. confidence as learners 6. attendance 7. discipline	• Student achievement • Student, parent, mentor, or administrator reflections (questionnaires or interviews) • Observation data • Participant portfolios (student) • Videos or audio tapes (instruction)	Program Improvement: all aspects of program design, professional development, and structure

✓ **Research to Practice Insight:** The Yearly Mentoring Activities Checklist (presented in Part III) could be reformatted and used by individual mentors or MCTs to record activities actually provided. Dates or initials could be recorded to track specific activities implemented. It could also be used as a way to generate data and discussion about the effectiveness of mentoring activities.

The resources provided in Part V allow Mentor Core Teams to understand, over time, the impact of their efforts on teacher turnover and on perceptions of support provided to new teachers. At the same time, several allow the Mentor Core Team and mentoring teachers to assess the program from their perspective. Select the assessment instruments that are most appropriate for your school. If necessary, tailor the instruments to your specific needs.

MCT IMPLEMENTATION AND IMPACT: SELF-ASSESSMENT RUBRIC

Purpose: To be used by the Mentor Core Team members as a tool for self-reflection to highlight their program's current stage of development and to identify areas for growth and development.

Timing: Annually, generally at the end of each school year.

Rank your MCT by the following stages for each program element listed below (Table 17.2).

- **Initiation Stage:** Implemented at a minimal level; awareness of importance; attempts to initiate; some impact; commitment by a few faculty members
- **Developing Stage:** Implemented at an appropriate level; progress is evident; some significant impact; some visible commitment
- **Sustaining Stage:** Implemented at a highly effective and institutionalized level; deeply embedded in policies, practices, and procedures; widespread impact; self-maintaining; strong commitment.

66 ——— A Comment From the Field ———

Until we took this self-assessment, we really did not realize how far we had progressed as a Mentor Core Team. While we're at the sustaining level on most items, we still feel we have much more to do! Maybe this should be called the "has-become-part-of-our-school-culture" level!

High School Lead Mentor

99

DATA COLLECTION

Table 17.2   MCT Implementation and Impact

Our Current Mentor Program:	*Initiation Stage*	*Developing Stage*	*Sustaining Stage*
1. Promotes a schoolwide understanding of and commitment to mentoring.			
2. Is driven by clearly articulated and commonly understood goals.			
3. Is coordinated by an active Mentor Core Team (MCT) composed of an administrator, a lead mentor, and qualified teacher mentors.			
4. Has defined expectations, roles, and responsibilities for all MCT members.			
5. Has defined criteria and procedures for mentor selection and assignments.			
6. Ensures new teacher understanding of and commitment to mentoring expectations.			
7. Is coordinated effectively to support new teachers.			
8. Promotes meaningful professional learning and schoolwide collaboration.			
9. Is allocated adequate time, resources, and support to perform mentoring responsibilities.			

(Continued)

DATA COLLECTION

Table 17.2 (Continued)

Our Mentor Core Team (MCT):	Initiation Stage	Developing Stage	Sustaining Stage
10. Includes operational guidelines and procedures to assure efficient meetings, effective problem solving, planning, and communication.			
11. Facilitates appropriate professional development for mentors based on identified needs.			
12 Uses New Teacher Needs Assessment data to prioritize mentoring activities and develop Individualized Induction Plans.			
13. Provides appropriate mentoring activities to meet new teachers' social, emotional, and professional needs.			
14. Assures mentors develop effective coaching strategies to promote new teachers' instructional effectiveness.			
15. Uses evaluation data to improve program results (e.g., new teacher and mentor perceptions of support, school's professional climate for learning, instructional practices in classrooms, student achievement, teacher retention, and teacher leadership capacity).			
16. Has a positive impact on school improvement priorities.			
17. Is valued and supported by the district office and linked to the systemwide improvement plan.			
18. Contributes to individual and facultywide professional sharing and growth, teacher leadership, and capacity building.			
19. Is structured to ensure continuous progress and sustainability.			
20. Celebrates and recognizes the contributions of mentors and the accomplishments of beginning teachers.			
Total Number of Elements	Initiation Stage _____	Developing Stage _____	Sustaining Stage _____

Please add any comments or suggestions that would help us in strengthening our current program.

Copyright © 2009 by Corwin Press. All rights reserved. Reprinted from *Mentoring as Collaboration:Lessons From the Field for Classroom, School, and District Leaders* by Mary Ann Blank and Cheryl A. Kershaw. Thousand Oaks, CA: Corwin Press, www.corwinpress.com. Reproduction authorized only for the local school site or nonprofit organization that has purchased this book.

MENTOR'S REFLECTION: SELF-ASSESSMENT

Purpose: To promote each mentor's reflection on elements of a high-quality coaching experience

Timing: Periodically throughout the mentorship

Table 17.3   Mentor's Reflection

Check the statements you feel are exhibited consistently and to a high degree.

	✓	*In my role as a Professional Role Model, Liaison, Facilitator, Relationship Builder, and Supporter to my protégé, have I . . .*
1.		Maintained a positive relationship characterized by openness and trust?
2.		Been accessible and available for frequent interactions and to answer questions needing immediate responses?
3.		Held scheduled conferences for progress checks to reinforce steps forward and to set goals for continued growth?
4.		Maintained confidentiality and followed through on my commitments and promises?
5.		Provided opportunities for productive collaboration with colleagues to enhance students' learning?
6.		Provided spontaneous, credible, and specific praise about personal or professional efforts and accomplishments?
7.		Modeled the importance of maintaining supportive professional relationships with colleagues?
8.		Demonstrated respect, accessibility, and expertise when engaging in dialogue with others (especially those from diverse home and community situations and cultures)?
9.		Modeled ethical professional behaviors and ensured understanding and implementation of laws related to students' rights and teacher responsibilities?
10.		Increased my protégé's knowledge and use of research-based instructional practices and the resources available for professional learning?

(Continued)

DATA COLLECTION

Table 17.3 (Continued)

DATA COLLECTION

	✓	*In my role as an Instructional Coach to my protégé, have I . . .*
11.		Sought to learn about cultures represented by our students and families and consistently modeled respect for diversity and culturally relevant instruction?
12.		Modeled my commitment to staying current in content and instructional approaches and actively pursued professional goals and personal renewal?
13.		Modeled professional attitudes and my desire to improve practice by seeking constructive suggestions and by responding positively to feedback?
14.		Provided clear corrective feedback and prioritized instructional recommendations that result in improved outcomes for students?
15.		Encouraged the development of his/her unique teaching style rather than an imitation of mine?
16.		Increased awareness of the connections between students' needs and abilities and instructional objectives, strategies, and assessments?
17.		Provided a model for reflection on teaching practice by examining assessments related to the academic performance of individuals and important subgroups?
18.		Modeled a process of problem solving that views the challenge from a variety of perspectives that lead to problem understanding and a range of possible solutions?
19.		Guided the process of identifying possible causes or intervening factors related to less than desired performance and ways to incorporate appropriate short- and long-term interventions?
20.		Prompted realistic reflections and self-assessments that result in improved outcomes for students?
21.		Increased feelings of self-efficacy, problem-solving ability, and flexibility in identifying alternative approaches?
22.		Celebrated my protégé's successes?

Copyright © 2009 by Corwin Press. All rights reserved. Reprinted from *Mentoring as Collaboration: Lessons From the Field for Classroom, School, and District Leaders* by Mary Ann Blank and Cheryl A. Kershaw. Thousand Oaks, CA: Corwin Press, www.corwinpress.com. Reproduction authorized only for the local school site or nonprofit organization that has purchased this book.

FORMATIVE MENTOR PROGRAM ASSESSMENT: NEW TEACHERS

Purpose: Use this formative assessment to gather information about the mentor/new teacher relationship so that needed changes and adjustments can be made.

Timing: Late fall or as needed

About the Mentor/New Teacher Relationship

1. In your opinion, your mentor/new teacher relationship is working

   _____ very well.

   _____ just fine.

   _____ not too well.

   _____ very badly.

2. If it is working well, what do you think are the reasons why?

3. If it is not working well, what is(are) the cause(s) of the problems?

4. What suggestions do you have to remedy the situation? What changes do you feel need to be made?

5. Would you like for us to discuss this in greater depth?

About the Mentoring Program

6. What have been the most positive or productive activities or opportunities of the program?

7. What have been any negative or unproductive activities or opportunities of the program?

8. What are your short- or long-term suggestions for improving the Mentoring Program?

Copyright © 2009 by Corwin Press. All rights reserved. Reprinted from *Mentoring as Collaboration:Lessons From the Field for Classroom, School, and District Leaders* by Mary Ann Blank and Cheryl A. Kershaw. Thousand Oaks, CA: Corwin Press, www.corwinpress.com. Reproduction authorized only for the local school site or nonprofit organization that has purchased this book.

DATA COLLECTION

FORMATIVE MENTOR PROGRAM ASSESSMENT: MENTORS

Purpose: Use this formative assessment to gather information about the mentor/new teacher relationship so that needed changes and adjustments can be made.

Timing: Late fall or as needed

About the Mentor/New Teacher Relationship

1. In your opinion, your mentor/new teacher relationship is working

   _____ very well.

   _____ just fine.

   _____ not too well.

   _____ very badly.

2. If it is working well, what do you think are the reasons why?

3. If it is not working well, what is(are) the cause(s) of the problems?

4. What suggestions do you have to remedy the situation? What changes do you feel need to be made?

5. Would you like for us to discuss this in greater depth?

About the Mentoring Program

6. What have been the most positive or productive activities or opportunities of the program?

7. What have been any negative or unproductive activities or opportunities of the program?

8. What are your short- or long-term suggestions for improving the Mentoring Program?

Copyright © 2009 by Corwin Press. All rights reserved. Reprinted from *Mentoring as Collaboration:Lessons From the Field for Classroom, School, and District Leaders* by Mary Ann Blank and Cheryl A. Kershaw. Thousand Oaks, CA: Corwin Press, www.corwinpress.com. Reproduction authorized only for the local school site or nonprofit organization that has purchased this book.

NEW TEACHER PERCEPTIONS OF THE MENTORING EXPERIENCE: ASSESSMENT

Purpose: Use this summative assessment to determine the effectiveness of all aspects of the Mentoring Program in addressing the needs of new teachers.

Timing: At the end of school each year

Table 17.4   Perceptions of the Mentoring Experience

Please rate the following components of our program in terms of their impact on your growth as a professional this year. Circle the number that most accurately reflects your perception for each statement. If you did not experience an item, circle "NA."

Scale:						
1 = Strongly Disagree	2 = Disagree		3 = Agree		4 = Strongly Agree	
Perceptions of the Mentoring Experience						
		Scale				
1. Mentors at my school helped me understand the professional expectations for teachers related to						
a. Fulfilling classroom responsibilities	1	2	3	4	NA	
b. Assuming grade-level or departmental responsibilities	1	2	3	4	NA	
c. Assuming appropriate school-level responsibilities (e.g., extracurricular, committees)	1	2	3	4	NA	
d. Knowing and following school/school system policies and procedures (e.g., paperwork, special education requirements, emergency procedures)	1	2	3	4	NA	
e. Addressing standards (national, state, system, INTASC)	1	2	3	4	NA	
f. Completing the Teacher Evaluation Process (e.g., professional expectations, evaluation criteria, paperwork, timelines)	1	2	3	4	NA	
2. Mentors helped me learn how to establish and maintain effective professional relationships						
a. With students	1	2	3	4	NA	
b. With parents and caregivers	1	2	3	4	NA	
c. With colleagues	1	2	3	4	NA	
d. With administrators and other school/school system leaders	1	2	3	4	NA	
e. With community members	1	2	3	4	NA	
3. Mentoring activities that helped me develop as an educator included						
a. Regularly scheduled conferences during the school day with mentor(s) to plan, discuss issues, or celebrate accomplishments	1	2	3	4	NA	
b. Informal conferences with mentor(s)	1	2	3	4	NA	

(Continued)

Table 17.4 (Continued)

Scale:						
1 = Strongly Disagree	2 = Disagree		3 = Agree		4 = Strongly Agree	

Perceptions of the Mentoring Experience

		Scale			
c. Coaching by my mentor (e.g., observations, promoting reflection, providing feedback, encouraging new strategies)	1	2	3	4	NA
d. Observing mentor(s) and other faculty members	1	2	3	4	NA
e. Informal meetings with other faculty	1	2	3	4	NA
f. Informal "get-togethers"	1	2	3	4	NA
g. Learning opportunities at the school (e.g., sharing of effective strategies, workshops, special sessions on topics of interest to new teachers, study groups)	1	2	3	4	NA
h. Encouragement to attend systemwide learning opportunities (e.g. in-service sessions, new teacher orientations, new teacher workshops)	1	2	3	4	NA
4. Mentors impacted my professional development by					
a. Serving as professional role models	1	2	3	4	NA
b. Accepting me as a professional colleague	1	2	3	4	NA
c. Making time for me when I needed assistance	1	2	3	4	NA
d. Providing the specific support and assistance I needed	1	2	3	4	NA
e. Listening to my concerns and helping me identify solutions	1	2	3	4	NA
f. Being flexible and open-minded in assisting me	1	2	3	4	NA
g. Helping me get to know other faculty and staff	1	2	3	4	NA
h. Linking me with faculty who could assist me in addressing my concerns	1	2	3	4	NA
i. Helping me acquire the resources I needed	1	2	3	4	NA
j. Helping me develop a repertoire of effective instructional strategies	1	2	3	4	NA
k. Helping me design a supportive learning environment and effective classroom management system	1	2	3	4	NA
l. Helping me learn strategies to address the diverse needs of my students	1	2	3	4	NA
m. Helping me develop interpersonal and relationship-building skills	1	2	3	4	NA
n. Helping me understand the organization and culture of the school	1	2	3	4	NA

DATA COLLECTION

	SD	D	A	SA	
o. Helping me understand the school community and its issues, strengths, and resources that impact our students	1	2	3	4	NA
p. Linking me with community resources that are available to address the diverse needs of my students	1	2	3	4	NA
q. Helping me learn to balance my own life responsibilities with the demands of teaching	1	2	3	4	NA
r. Helping me become a more reflective teacher	1	2	3	4	NA
s. Making me aware of my development as an educator and assisting me in setting goals for my continued professional growth.	1	2	3	4	NA

DATA COLLECTION

Please complete the sentence stems below. Be as specific as possible, including examples, and write on the back of this survey if you need additional space.

1. I most appreciate the Mentoring Program and/or my mentor for . . .

2. The Mentoring Program addressed my specific needs as a new teacher by . . .

3. The Mentoring Program has impacted my professional development as a teacher by . . .

4. My suggestions for improving the Mentoring Program would be:

Copyright © 2009 by Corwin Press. All rights reserved. Reprinted from *Mentoring as Collaboration: Lessons From the Field for Classroom, School, and District Leaders* by Mary Ann Blank and Cheryl A. Kershaw. Thousand Oaks, CA: Corwin Press, www.corwinpress.com. Reproduction authorized only for the local school site or nonprofit organization that has purchased this book.

SUMMATIVE MENTOR PROGRAM ASSESSMENT: MENTORS

Purpose: This summative survey is designed for mentors to share their perceptions about the overall effectiveness of the Mentoring Program and their suggestions for improvement.

Timing: At the end of school each year

Please rate each statement using the following scale:

1= Strongly Disagree   2 = Disagree   3 = Agree   4 = Strongly Agree

As a mentor working with the new teacher, I felt . . .

1. The relationship we had was positive.   1   2   3   4

2. The relationship I had with the Lead Mentor was positive.   1   2   3   4

3. My responsibilities as a mentor were clearly communicated.   1   2   3   4

4. My responsibilities as a mentor were appropriate and realistic. 1   2   3   4

5. The assistance I was able to provide to the new teacher was
   of benefit.   1   2   3   4

6. The time I had to perform mentoring responsibilities
   was adequate.   1   2   3   4

7. The assistance and training I received was helpful.   1   2   3   4

8. The new teacher clearly understood his/her responsibilities.   1   2   3   4

9. The new teacher responded professionally/positively
   to my suggestions.   1   2   3   4

10. The new teacher showed adequate growth in
    fulfilling expectations.   1   2   3   4

11. The new teacher now has the skills/attitude to be an
    effective teacher.   1   2   3   4

12. Any problems were resolved constructively and professionally. 1   2   3   4

13. The mentoring program was well organized and smoothly run. 1   2   3   4

14. What I like best about being a mentor is . . .

15. Suggestions I have about improving the mentoring experience/program are . . .

16. I will participate in the Mentoring Program next year.   Yes / No

    My reasons are . . .

Copyright © 2009 by Corwin Press. All rights reserved. Reprinted from *Mentoring as Collaboration:Lessons From the Field for Classroom, School, and District Leaders* by Mary Ann Blank and Cheryl A. Kershaw. Thousand Oaks, CA: Corwin Press, www.corwinpress.com. Reproduction authorized only for the local school site or nonprofit organization that has purchased this book.

SUMMATIVE MENTOR PROGRAM ASSESSMENT: NEW TEACHERS

Purpose: This summative survey allows new teachers to share their perceptions of the overall effectiveness of the Mentoring Program and their suggestions for improvement.

Timing: At the end of school each year

Please rate each statement using the following scale:

1= Strongly Disagree   2 = Disagree   3 = Agree   4 = Strongly Agree   "NA" = Did Not Experience

As a new teacher working with mentoring teachers, I felt . . .

1. The relationship I had with my mentor was positive.   **1   2   3   4   NA**

2. The relationship I had with the Lead Mentor was positive. **1   2   3   4   NA**

3. My responsibilities as a new teacher were clearly communicated.   **1   2   3   4   NA**

4. My responsibilities as a new teacher were appropriate and realistic.   **1   2   3   4   NA**

5. The assistance and support I received from my mentor was of benefit.   **1   2   3   4   NA**

6. The assistance and support I received from the principal was of benefit.   **1   2   3   4   NA**

7. The assistance and support I received from other faculty was of benefit.   **1   2   3   4   NA**

8. The time with my mentor was adequate for planning, conferencing, etc.   **1   2   3   4   NA**

9. The professional development (induction) opportunities were helpful.   **1   2   3   4   NA**

10. My mentor clearly understood and fulfilled his/her responsibilities.   **1   2   3   4   NA**

11. My mentor was professional and positive in dealing with me.   **1   2   3   4   NA**

12. I was able to show adequate growth in fulfilling expectations.   **1   2   3   4   NA**

13. I now have the skills and attitude to an effective teacher.   **1   2   3   4   NA**

14. Any problems were resolved constructively and professionally.   **1   2   3   4   NA**

15. The mentoring program was well organized and ran smoothly   **1   2   3   4   NA**

16. What I liked best about my mentor was . . .

17. Suggestions I have about making the mentoring experience better are . . .

18. Would you like to receive mentoring assistance next year?   Yes / No

Copyright © 2009 by Corwin Press. All rights reserved. Reprinted from *Mentoring as Collaboration: Lessons From the Field for Classroom, School, and District Leaders* by Mary Ann Blank and Cheryl A. Kershaw. Thousand Oaks, CA: Corwin Press, www.corwinpress.com. Reproduction authorized only for the local school site or nonprofit organization that has purchased this book.

DATA COLLECTION

TEAMWORK: SELF-ASSESSMENT

Purpose: MCT members are to complete this self-assessment (Table 17.5) to determine how the team functions compared to the following attributes of high-performing teams. The Lead Mentor could summarize the responses to identify and reinforce the most consistent attributes and engage the team in setting goals to improve priority attributes that are less consistently exhibited.

Timing: Use as a formative assessment (sometime in November) and as a summative assessment (near the end of the year).

Table 17.5 Attributes of High-Performing Teams

Mentor Core Team Members	Always	Often	Some-times	Hardly Ever or Never
1. Are conscientious in accomplishing roles and assigned responsibilities				
2: Are fully committed to our goal of helping new teachers succeed				
3. Are fully committed to helping new teachers and each other				
4. Exhibit productive collaborative behaviors and skills: • are present, on time, and ready to go • are focused on our agenda • capitalize on the talents of our members • offer creative, and sometimes counter, suggestions to challenge the status quo • resolve situations or conflicts constructively				
5. Make decisions based on our primary criterion of what is best for our students (then on our secondary criterion of what is best for our new teachers)				
6. Follow established procedures when corrective action is required				
7. Adhere to our rule of confidentiality in all matters regarding new teachers or mentors				
8. Exhibit self-directed learning behaviors by engaging in ongoing professional development as mentors and teacher leaders				
9. Are willing to assess program impact related with a focus on students and their learning opportunities				
10. Recognize, utilize, and celebrate the expertise of colleagues				

Copyright © 2009 by Corwin Press. All rights reserved. Reprinted from *Mentoring as Collaboration: Lessons From the Field for Classroom, School, and District Leaders* by Mary Ann Blank and Cheryl A. Kershaw. Thousand Oaks, CA: Corwin Press, www.corwinpress.com. Reproduction authorized only for the local school site or nonprofit organization that has purchased this book.

Discussion Starters:

☛ At this point, one especially productive team behavior we exhibit is . . . ?

☛ In the future, to be a higher-performing team, one behavior we need to improve on is . . .

NEW TEACHER FOCUS GROUP: INTERVIEW QUESTIONS

Purpose: Using a formative focus group interview process provides an opportunity for new teachers to share their perceptions of learning to teach at your school. It also gives them an opportunity to affirm the most effective aspects of your Mentor Program and to suggest areas for growth. Use the questions provided, or adapt them to your own context. Compile and share the responses—and use them for fine-tuning your program. Celebrate and share the "success stories"!

Timing: At the end of school each year

Possible Questions:

1. What do you see as the greatest needs of new teachers in your school during

   a. the beginning of school?

   b. the first year overall?

   c. the second and third years?

2. In what ways has the mentoring you have received helped you with

   a. Developing supportive relationships and a positive classroom climate?

   b. Establishing an effective classroom management system?

   c. Improving student learning or motivation to learn in your classroom?

   d. Using effective instructional strategies to address the needs of diverse learners in your classroom?

3. Do you have some "success stories" that you would like to share?

4. What do you see as the major challenges in continuing to develop the school's Mentor Program?

5. Is there anything else related to your Mentor Program that you would like to share?

Copyright © 2009 by Corwin Press. All rights reserved. Reprinted from *Mentoring as Collaboration: Lessons From the Field for Classroom, School, and District Leaders* by Mary Ann Blank and Cheryl A. Kershaw. Thousand Oaks, CA: Corwin Press, www.corwinpress.com. Reproduction authorized only for the local school site or nonprofit organization that has purchased this book.

DATA COLLECTION

MENTOR FOCUS GROUP: INTERVIEW QUESTIONS

Purpose: Using a formative focus group interview process provides an opportunity for mentors to share their perceptions of coaching new teachers at your school. It also gives them an opportunity to affirm the most effective aspects of your Mentor Program and to suggest areas for growth. Use the questions provided or adapt them to your own context. Compile and share the responses—and use them for fine-tuning your program. Celebrate and share the "success stories"!

Timing: At the end of school each year

Possible Questions:

1. What do you see as the greatest needs of new teachers in your school during

   a. the beginning of school?

   b. the first year overall?

   c. the second and third years?

2. In what ways has your Mentor Program promoted supportive relationships and a positive school climate?

3. In what ways has mentoring increased the level of student learning and motivation to learn in your classroom?

4. In what ways has mentoring increased appropriate student behavior and overall classroom management in your classroom?

5. In what ways has mentoring increased the use of effective instructional strategies to address the needs of diverse learners in your classroom?

6. Have you had some "success stories" for your Mentor Program that you would like to share?

7. What do you see as the next steps for growth of your school's Mentor Program? (Building on successes, addressing challenges)

8. Is there anything else related to your Mentor Program that you would like to share?

Copyright © 2009 by Corwin Press. All rights reserved. Reprinted from *Mentoring as Collaboration:Lessons From the Field for Classroom, School, and District Leaders* by Mary Ann Blank and Cheryl A. Kershaw. Thousand Oaks, CA: Corwin Press, www.corwinpress.com. Reproduction authorized only for the local school site or nonprofit organization that has purchased this book.

DATA COLLECTION

TRACKING TEACHER ATTRITION AND MOBILITY: DOCUMENTATION RECORD

School _____

School Year _____

Purpose: Tracking teacher attrition and mobility (see Table 17.6) provides important data about the effectiveness of your Mentor Program in attracting _and keeping_ talented teachers on your faculty. This provides an essential data source for school improvement planning and for systemwide improvement efforts. Knowing WHY teachers are leaving provides a far more complete picture of teacher attrition than simply calculating percentages.

Timing: By the last day of school at the end of each year

Table 17.6   Teacher Attrition and Mobility Self-Assessment

Directions: Identify each teacher who left by initials in the box that reflects the level of experience and the reason for leaving.

	New Teachers < 3 Years Experience & Nontenured			Experienced Teachers > 3 Years Experience & Tenured		
Retirement						
Move or change of location						
Teacher-requested transfer to another school (same level)						
Teacher-requested transfer to another school (different level)						
Teacher-initiated change to a private school						
Family issues (marriage, pregnancy, caregiving)						
Illness						
Administrative move (principal transfers teacher)						
Resignation						
Nonrenewal of contract						
Change of role within school or system						
Change of role to another system or school in another system						
Other (specify)						

Copyright © 2009 by Corwin Press. All rights reserved. Reprinted from _Mentoring as Collaboration: Lessons From the Field for Classroom, School, and District Leaders_ by Mary Ann Blank and Cheryl A. Kershaw. Thousand Oaks, CA: Corwin Press, www.corwinpress.com. Reproduction authorized only for the local school site or nonprofit organization that has purchased this book.

DATA COLLECTION

EXIT QUESTIONNAIRE: SAMPLE FORM

Purpose: To be used by school Lead Mentors or district mentor coordinators to determine the reasons and influences for teacher mobility or attrition and to inform schools and districts about needed improvements in the quality of school life to attract and retain teachers. This questionnaire (Table 17.7) could be online to ensure confidentiality.

Timing: When teachers request a change in the status of their employment

Demographics:
Years of experience: ____ 0–3 ____ 4–7 ____ 8–15 ____ 16+
Characteristics of assigned school: ____ Urban ____ Suburban
                                    ____ Rural ____ Other
School level: ____ Pre-K ____ Primary ____ Intermediate ____ MS ____ HS

Table 17.7 Sample Exit Questionnaire

What was (were) the specific reason(s) for your decision to leave your current school assignment? Please check all that apply.

Reasons	*Please Check*
Retirement	
Move or change of residence	
Teacher-requested transfer to another school (same level)	
Teacher-requested transfer to another school (different level)	
Teacher-initiated change to a private school	
Family issues (marriage, pregnancy, caregiving, other)	
Illness	
Administrative move (principal transfers teacher)	
Resignation	
Nonrenewal of contract	
Change of role (within school or system)	
Change of role to another system or school in another system	
Other (please specify)	

At this time, do you feel that your absence will be permanent or temporary? Please explain.

What were the major influences in your decision to not teach in your current school next year? Please check all that apply.

	Please Check
Personal	
Demands of teaching incompatible with my life	
Excessive time demands in non-school hours	
Limited intellectual challenge	
Unsatisfying interpersonal relationships	
Misalignment of personal expectations with realities of teaching	
Desire to try other career opportunities	
Change in personal life situation (marriage, pregnancy, move)	
Economic	
Adequacy of salary	
Adequacy of benefits	
Attractiveness of earning opportunities in other careers	
Current location's cost of living	
Excessive out-of-pocket expenditures to enhance learning	
Professional	
Excessive work demands	
Lack of professional control	
Low professional prestige	
Limited opportunity for advancement as a teacher	
Limited opportunities for professional development	
Limited resources	
Excessive requirements beyond teaching	
School-related	
Excessive work load (multiple preparations, challenging students, extracurricular demands)	
Communication issues (being informed, collaborating with colleagues, working with families)	
Inadequate working conditions (teaching assignments)	
Safety and security concerns	
Inadequate facilities, equipment, or resources	
Student discipline and motivational challenges	
Lack of professional support (from administration, colleagues, mentor, parents)	

Copyright © 2009 by Corwin Press. All rights reserved. Reprinted from *Mentoring as Collaboration:Lessons From the Field for Classroom, School, and District Leaders* by Mary Ann Blank and Cheryl A. Kershaw. Thousand Oaks, CA: Corwin Press, www.corwinpress.com. Reproduction authorized only for the local school site or nonprofit organization that has purchased this book.

DATA COLLECTION

DATA COLLECTION

COLLECTING STUDENT DATA: GUIDELINES

Purpose: To assist mentors in working with new teachers and to assess the overall impact of the Mentor Program in promoting student achievement.

Timing: Mentors could use this list of data sources with their new teachers at any time. The Mentor Core Team should gather data at the end of each semester or year to use in making decisions about the appropriateness of their plans and activities in promoting the quality of teaching and learning that result in increased student learning and motivation to learn.

Academic Data Sources

- Grades
- Test Scores
- Student Portfolios
- Performance Assessments (Rubrics)
- Student Self-Assessments (Individual and Group)
- Performance of students in various ability-level groups
- Analyzing the performance of students by ability level
- Analyzing the performance of students by ability groups

✓ **Research to Practice Insight:** Analyzing student performance by ability groups raises new teachers' awareness of the need to differentiate instruction to meet the needs of ALL students. This is not easy to do by just looking over the grade book. Help develop a chart that will enable them to gather and use this important information as it fits their grade level or course. Use a chart similar to the one below to help them identify ways to better address the needs of students who are underperforming—at any level.

Teacher: Mrs. Nickels							9th Grade English
	Initial Grades	Unit 1	Paper 1	Unit 2	Project	Paper 2	Notes
High							
Student Name							
Student Name							
Student Name							
Average							
Student Name							
Student Name							
Student Name							
Low							
Student Name							
Student Name							
Student Name							

Copyright © 2009 by Corwin Press. All rights reserved. Reprinted from *Mentoring as Collaboration:Lessons From the Field for Classroom, School, and District Leaders* by Mary Ann Blank and Cheryl A. Kershaw. Thousand Oaks, CA: Corwin Press, www.corwinpress.com. Reproduction authorized only for the local school site or nonprofit organization that has purchased this book.

Behavioral Data Sources

- *Tracking Discipline Referrals/Behavior Problems.* Use charts such as the one below (Table 17.8) to help new teachers understand patterns of student misbehavior. The Mentor Core Team could track improvements in student behavior as new teachers gain experience and/or design professional development sessions to address identified problem areas.

Table 17.8   Discipline Problems/Referrals

Date	Student	Male/Female	A.M. / P.M.	Reason(s)

Copyright © 2009 by Corwin Press. All rights reserved. Reprinted from *Mentoring as Collaboration: Lessons From the Field for Classroom, School, and District Leaders* by Mary Ann Blank and Cheryl A. Kershaw. Thousand Oaks, CA: Corwin Press, www.corwinpress.com. Reproduction authorized only for the local school site or nonprofit organization that has purchased this book.

- *Student Questionnaires or Interviews.* Help beginning teachers learn to ask students to share their perceptions of behavior in the classroom. What is helping them behave well? What is getting in the way? Refer to student feedback in both mentoring and planning.
- *Family or Caregiver Contacts.* Help new teachers keep a log of parent communication to be used in reflecting on their own performance (see Table 17.9). Have them share patterns of parental and student responses with the Mentor Core Team as a formative assessment. Use compiled feedback from new teachers to guide informal discussions or formal professional development sessions on topics such as engaging families and preparing for parent meetings.

Table 17.9   Family Contacts

Student/Contact	Date	Compliment or Concern Shared	Contact's Response	Resulting Student Behavior

Copyright © 2009 by Corwin Press. All rights reserved. Reprinted from *Mentoring as Collaboration: Lessons From the Field for Classroom, School, and District Leaders* by Mary Ann Blank and Cheryl A. Kershaw. Thousand Oaks, CA: Corwin Press, www.corwinpress.com. Reproduction authorized only for the local school site or nonprofit organization that has purchased this book.

Perceptions of Classroom Climate

- *Questionnaires.* At transition points such as after the first few weeks of school, at the semester, or at the end of the year, encourage beginning teachers (and mentors) to ask students for feedback regarding classroom climate. Use the information to help new teachers make needed changes to assure a warm, businesslike learning environment. Allowing students to respond anonymously will assure the new teacher that the feedback is honest! The following classroom climate interviews have been used in working with students at all grade levels.

DATA COLLECTION

DATA COLLECTION

PRIMARY STUDENT
CLASSROOM CLIMATE: SURVEY

1. My teacher is nice to me.

2. My teacher helps me learn
   new things.

3. My teacher answers my questions.

4. Students in my class are nice to
   each other.

5. I know how to behave in school.

6. I like coming to school.

Here is a picture of what I like best about school . . . .

Source: Blank & Kershaw (1998).

ELEMENTARY STUDENT CLASSROOM CLIMATE: SURVEY

Circle "Yes" or "No"

1. My teacher is nice to me.		Yes	No
2. My teacher helps me learn new things.		Yes	No
3. My teacher answers my questions or helps me find the answers.		Yes	No
4. My teacher helps me with my problems.		Yes	No
5. Students in my class are nice to each other.		Yes	No
6. Students in my class follow the teacher's directions.		Yes	No
7. Students in my class help each other learn.		Yes	No
8. What I am learning is interesting to me.		Yes	No
9. I know how to behave in school.		Yes	No
10. I know how to study and learn.		Yes	No
11. I can make choices about what I learn.		Yes	No
12. My teacher listens when I have something important to say.		Yes	No
13. I have friends at school.		Yes	No
14. I like coming to school.		Yes	No

15. What I like best about my class is _____

_____

_____

16. What I'd like to change about class is _____

_____

_____

Source: Blank & Kershaw (1998).

DATA COLLECTION

MIDDLE AND HIGH SCHOOL STUDENT CLASSROOM CLIMATE: SURVEY

Please mark the appropriate square that best describes your experience. Feel free to use the back of this survey to include comments or suggestions.

	Strongly Agree	Agree	Disagree	Strongly Disagree
For me, the atmosphere in this classroom:				
is cooperative	O	O	O	O
is encouraging	O	O	O	O
is friendly	O	O	O	O
is supportive and caring	O	O	O	O
lets me be myself	O	O	O	O
is fair	O	O	O	O
encourages me to learn	O	O	O	O
is safe and relaxing	O	O	O	O
allows me to share my opinions and ideas	O	O	O	O
For me, the classwork and/or homework:				
is neither too easy nor too hard	O	O	O	O
is stimulating (neither boring nor busywork)	O	O	O	O
is new and interesting	O	O	O	O
is of use to me	O	O	O	O
is challenging	O	O	O	O
My teacher:				
is willing to give me extra time	O	O	O	O
shows understanding	O	O	O	O
gives clear directions and helps me understand	O	O	O	O
tests and grades fairly	O	O	O	O
is willing to help with my problems	O	O	O	O
recognizes my accomplishments	O	O	O	O
uses group work to help us learn more	O	O	O	O

Source: Blank & Kershaw (1998).

18

How to Use Data for Program Improvement

The most effective Mentor Programs credit their long-term approach and use of data to make annual refinements as the essential keys to their growth and development. One exceptional Mentor Core Team tells all preservice and new in-service teachers that "It's all about our students. They come first. You come second—as you are still learning to teach in our school. The rest of us are working for you both." By making this statement overt, they have been able to make numerous changes in their school culture. First, mentors have to apply to mentor and be selected. If their mentoring assignments need to be altered for any reason, they accept it because the focus is on the new teacher. Second, school administrators and experienced teachers, many of them serving as mentors, no longer assign beginning teachers to "float," to teach three different classes, or to assume too many additional responsibilities. With the induction program squarely focused on students first, they make sure that the new teachers are not given overwhelming work expectations.

Outcomes such as these are not the result of "hoped for" planning. These schools have built their programs around clearly defined plans and the use of formative data to guide their development. The teacher leaders who have taken ownership of their programs have had to overcome the fear of being told that aspects of their programs are not being perceived as they had intended. They have identified problem areas and worked together to design, implement, and assess their solutions. They have also had to learn that it is as important to celebrate successes as it is to focus on what needs to be improved. Overall, they have learned valuable lessons about organizational growth and development that is frequently beyond the realm of classroom teachers. This is why they become such advocates of building learning communities. They have learned how to improve their schools and their student outcomes by monitoring their continuous progress and planning for sustainability as they have helped their beginning teachers flourish.

USING MENTORING DATA TO IDENTIFY SCHOOL AND SYSTEM IMPROVEMENT PRIORITIES: GUIDELINES

The Mentor Core Team should develop an annual action plan with revisions based on data gathered from the sources indicated earlier in the chapter. More important, however, is that this plan be perceived as a central component of the school improvement planning process. Mentoring is clearly correlated to improving student achievement—the bottom line for any school. Sanders and Horn (1998), reporting on an analysis of value-added data, identified teachers as the most important factor in impacting student achievement. According to Sanders (personal communication, February 2, 2004), it takes approximately three to five years for novice teachers, even those among the most effective, to produce significant gains in student achievement. Furthermore, he has concluded that if students have a low-performing teacher for two years in a row, it becomes extremely difficult for those students to overcome the resulting deficits in their learning curves, which ultimately impacts their success in school. Therefore, students' academic potential is adversely impacted by the revolving door of new teachers who leave their classrooms and the profession before they have developed the level of expertise needed to promote their learning (Darling-Hammond, 2003). This is particularly acute in urban schools where the teacher attrition rates often exceed fifty percent (Howey, 2000; Ingersoll, 2001; NEA, 2004). As Cochran-Smith states, "teaching quality matters" (2003, p. 3). In describing a school system's innovative approach to improving student achievement by allowing a team of teachers to redesign schooling experiences for high-poverty children, Haycock (2005) concluded, "It will take schools organized to attract and support such teachers, schools of education organized to produce more of them, and policies to provide the necessary support" to see widespread gains in student achievement (p. 262).

Effective mentor programs, whether at the school or district level, have clearly articulated action steps, persons responsible, timelines, resources needed, and funding sources. Their goals all address improving student achievement by strengthening teacher quality through mentoring. The plans assure that all beginning teachers and mentoring teachers are supported effectively and are changed, midstream, if this is not happening. They also change from year to year as the Mentor Core Team reflects on successes and addresses challenges. Over time, the most effective MCTs have built a solid structure for supporting beginning teachers and begun to expand their focus to strengthening the knowledge, skills, and dispositions of all faculty members. In numerous cases, we have seen the MCTs become the formal catalyst for professional development in their schools. They provide the quality professional development that researchers and professional organizations are calling for— research-based learning, often action research, embedded in the context of the school and classroom that develops teacher leadership capacity for changing day-to-day practice to improve student learning (Lambert, 2003; Moir and Bloom, 2003; NEA Foundation for the Improvement of Education, 2002). In essence, they are developing the "experts among us."

The following are partial examples of school (see Table 18.1) and district (Table 18.2) induction plans that are integrated into both school and districtwide improvement plans. In reality, the plans contain additional details for each action step. Only the major action steps are included in the examples.

—— Comments From the Field ——

We were so excited about making our Mentor Program one of the best that we left the initial two days of training and went back to our schools full of ideas that we wanted to implement immediately. Believe it or not, we were able to put most of them into action in the first semester! We were exhausted, but very proud of our efforts.

At the end of the first semester, we surveyed our new teachers. What we found was that they truly appreciated our determination to mentor them effectively, but were overwhelmed with all that we were doing. When they told us that they felt they had to attend too many "30-Minute Thursday Sessions"—although they were all good ones—our feelings were initially dampened. When we stepped back and explored their responses a bit more, we realized that it wasn't just those sessions. It was those sessions in addition to everything else we were doing.

Once we realized that we were wearing everyone out, we asked the new teachers to help us identify the most important elements of our program for the first semester and what needed to be added or changed for second semester. After two years, we have now revamped our program a bit more and have developed a two-year approach by following the same process. Our program is much more effective now, the new teachers who started with us as we designed the program are now serving in leadership roles, and no one is overwhelmed. We also know that we will continue to refine what we are doing. It is just how we do business in our school.

Second-Year Mentor Core Team

Our Mentor Program has evolved into the catalyst for transforming our school into a learning community. When we started our mentoring program six years ago, we made typical structural decisions about who, how, when, and where. In our first year we assigned a primary mentor to each new teacher who was in the teacher's same department and a "professional associate" who was from a totally different field. We developed roles for each and the MCT provided training to assure they could carry out their roles. The professional associates were asked to focus on the new teachers' socialization and problem solving primarily. Mentors focused more on teaching and learning.

After the first year, our new teachers completed anonymous questionnaires about our program. Among other things, they told us that they liked having the professional associates as well as the mentors, but thought they could learn more from them. We used their feedback to enhance the roles of our professional associates who now encourage the new teachers to observe them teaching, schedule observations in other teachers' classrooms, and help them reflect on their required videotaped class sessions.

The Mentor Core Team has gathered feedback from mentors and beginning teachers every year and used what they have learned to strengthen the program. They have created a culture of sharing and have modeled using data to inform practice. We've been using their model for all of our professional development which they are now coordinating and which has been transformed from the traditional "in-service" approach to "collaboration meetings" focused on identified needs to reach their department's goals. Our teachers are leading their own professional development now. That's just one example of how we've used our mentor program data to grow our faculty—new and experienced!

High School Principal

Table 18.1   Sample School Action Plan (Partial)

Goal: To improve student achievement by assuring a smooth transition to teaching for all preservice teachers, new in-service teachers, and experienced teachers new to our school.				
Action Steps	*Person Responsible*	*Timeline*	*Required Resources*	*Funding Sources*
Include the induction program requirement in applicant's interviews	Principal and Mentor Core Team members	Summer or as needed	None	NA
Refine mentor plan for: (1) preservice teachers; (2) first-year teachers; (3) second-year teachers; (4) teachers new to our school	Mentor Core Team	Annually, late summer/early fall (based on spring feedback and new hires)	• Time for MCT to plan	NA
Assign each teacher a mentor and a professional associate	Mentor Core Team	Summer	None	NA
Develop and implement a new teacher orientation and handbook	Mentor Core Team	Summer before school orientation	• Food • Materials • Stipends for noncontract days	School Mentor Program Budget
Conduct annual preassessments	Lead Mentor	Orientation (two days before school starts)	• Preassessment instruments or Web site instructions	NA
Plan and implement Fall Orientation	Mentor Core Team and administrator	Spring (initial planning) Summer (final planning)	• Teacher Handbooks • Agendas • Faculty members to participate • Breakfast and lunch	School Mentor Program Budget
Organize "Forums" for Fall semester	Mentor Core Team	Summer	• MCT Meeting to revise forum schedule as needed • Faculty members to agree to conduct specific forums	NA
Meet with mentors to review mentoring practices and policies	Mentor Core Team	Fall	• Mentoring Policies (district) • Observing and providing feedback materials • Preparing for the evaluation process	School Mentor Program Budget

Goal: To improve student achievement by assuring a smooth transition to teaching for all preservice teachers, new in-service teachers, and experienced teachers new to our school.

Action Steps	Person Responsible	Timeline	Required Resources	Funding Sources
Meet with professional associates to review practices	Mentor Core Team	Fall	• Analyzing video reflections materials	NA
Conduct monthly "Forums"	Mentor Core Team and designated faculty	Monthly	• Varies depending on the specific forum • Materials • Duplication • Supplies for faculty conducting sessions	School Mentor Program Budget
Plan and implement fall "get-togethers"	Designated faculty member	2 per semester (or more if desired)	• Food • Supplies	School Mentor Program Budget
Schedule and implement bimonthly informal meetings	Designated faculty members	2 per month	• Food	School Mentor Program Budget
Mid-Year evaluation	Mentor Core Team	December	• Food • Library scheduled for online assessment	School Mentor Program Budget

Table 18.2   Sample District Action Plan (Partial)

Goals: To improve teacher quality; to attract and retain talented teachers in every school and classroom.				
Action Steps	*Person Responsible*	*Timeline*	*Required Resources*	*Funding Sources*
Establish a trained Mentor Core Team in every school in the district	Supervisor of Professional Development, Principals	Fall	• School mentoring funds • Stipends for Lead Mentors	PD Budget
Provide Training on an annual basis for new MCT and teachers or administrators added to the original team • Identify number of participants • Schedule two-day introductory training	Supervisor of Professional Development, Program trainers	Fall–Spring	• Handbooks • Presenters Materials • Substitute teachers • Location • Access to computer	PD Budget
Collect and analyze teacher turnover data from each MCT	Assistant to the Supervisor of Professional Development	Collect from principals in spring (before check out) Analysis—summer Report—fall	• Time • Computer skills	None
Conduct preassessments of beginning teachers at each school; analyze and report patterns to Supervisor of Professional Development	MCT Lead Mentor at each school, Principal	Early fall	• Time • Preassessments • Online survey software and development	None
Collect and analyze school data and report summary to superintendent	Supervisor of Professional Development	Early fall	• Time • Web design	
Begin development of Web-based assessments	Supervisor of Professional Development	August–July	• Time • Technology • Professional development of online surveys	PD Budget University technology department
Conduct postassessments of beginning teachers at each school	MCT Lead Mentors (conduct)	Distribute—April, Complete—May 15 Analyze and prepare summary June–July	• Time • Technology	PD Budget University technology department

Goals: To improve teacher quality; to attract and retain talented teachers in every school and classroom.				
Action Steps	*Person Responsible*	*Timeline*	*Required Resources*	*Funding Sources*
Collect and analyze postassessment data from all schools and report summary to superintendent	Supervisor of Professional Development and Assistant	May–August	• Time	NA
Develop ongoing advanced professional development for MCT members and system supervisors who are serving as external mentors	Supervisor of Professional Development	One day at opening of school, one meeting day per semester	• Computer access in each school • Professional development training materials and consultants ($.....)	PD budget, University faculty

19

How to Address Challenges and Celebrate Successes

Growing teacher mentoring and induction programs requires an honest, data-based appraisal of "what is" and a collective vision of "what ought to be." This is what separates mentoring programs that Jim Collins (2001) would celebrate as "great" programs versus those designated as "good" or well intentioned. The tendency of all conscientious mentors and Mentor Core Teams is to focus on what is not working as well as desired, not on celebrating successes. The following are ideas that affirm the hard work of mentoring and of learning to teach. Add others for both the school and district levels.

- Use some Mentor Core Team meetings to share mentoring success stories.
- Meet informally with new teachers to share success stories.
- Take time to acknowledge even small successes—face to face.
- Write personalized thank you messages.
- Include notes or articles in classroom or school newsletters or on the Web site.
- Include articles in districtwide publications or on the Web site.
- Say "thank you" with food!
- Give small mementos with the school logo or vision statement—or personalized.
- Hold a "Recognition Program" at the end of the year.
- Cover registration fees for an appropriate professional development activity.
- Provide stipends to compensate for time required for training events and mentoring activities.

- Provide unexpected public or private presentation of roses to individuals who have contributed to mentoring in some positive way.
- Encourage public support from the superintendent and school board.

---

66 ———————————— **A Comment From the Field** ————————————

We've been so focused on making sure that our new teachers are teaching effectively—as soon as possible—that we've switched from having happy hours or parties each month to "forums." The forums are great, too, but we have to let everyone get to know one another in more informal and less academic settings. Next semester, we're adding socialization back into our plan. Relationships and having some fun are just too important in this challenging work we do.

Middle School Mentor Core Team Member

99

Part V

Growing and Sustaining Your Mentor Program

The process of designing or redesigning your teacher mentor program has hopefully led to important modifications in the support provided to new teachers, additional or revised structures, and strategies that have shown a significant return on your investment of time and energy. Educators who are fortunate to work in collaborative professional cultures or learning communities understand that they have created something special.

“ —— A Comment From the Field ——

The outcomes of school-based mentoring we've seen are multifaceted—the impact extends beyond the novice teacher to experienced faculty as well. Our mentors definitely grow professionally as they incorporate research-based practices into their own classrooms, but the collaboration, sharing of expertise, and use of data to inform practice also contributes to the development of learning communities in our schools

The Authors

”

They experience many benefits not only from their new understandings about teaching and learning and their new strategies for reaching their students and partnering with families but also—most important—from the professional relationships nurtured in these schools. These are the schools that all teachers deserve—and must have if they are expected to raise the bar for student achievement. The teacher mentor program has been and can be the foundation for the development of many other professional learning communities in the school that use data, research, and collaboration to move beyond the status quo to higher levels of performance. Once the structures and strategies are in place, teachers will not go back to the isolating and professionally limiting "old way of doing business."

We believe in the motivational adage, "Nothing succeeds like success." Effective mentor programs lead to success for new teachers, mentors, and experienced faculty members and, as a result, stimulate continuous improvement, greater interest in research and data-based professional development, and sustainability.

We follow the advice of respected researchers, such as Schmoker (2004), who states "the most promising practice for sustained, substantive school improvement is building the capacity of school personnel to function as a Professional Learning Community" (p. 424). Educational leaders at all levels need to advocate for conditions that allow teachers to grow as teacher leaders in ways that promote the establishment of Professional Learning Communities. However, to be able to do this, they must first have hands-on experience with collaborative, teacher-led professional learning—and school-based mentoring is a place to start. Such experiences enhance collaboration by providing what Langer, Colton, & Goff (2003) describe as regular conversations about issues relevant to the new teacher's work. Richard Sagor (2003) finds optimism in these times of high expectations for universal student success and high-stakes accountability from working as colleagues in learning communities.

20

How to Promote Continuous Improvement

*Continuous Improvement Steps
and Feedback Loop*

In Part IV, we described effective mentoring professional development in relationship to Guskey's (2002) five levels of quality, which range from the lowest level of assessing participants' reactions to the highest level of impacting student outcomes. We strongly believe, and research has clearly documented, that analyzing the impact of school and district professional development on teacher and student outcomes is essential if professional development is to be transformed from the traditional smorgasbord of interesting and stimulating sessions into the catalyst for developing communities of learners. Building the competence, confidence, and "buy in" of all educators to change practices to improve student outcomes requires that school and district leaders rethink professional development—making it an essential and thoughtfully designed component of the continuous improvement cycle. Data-based decisions should drive the selection of professional development needed to address clearly defined targeted outcomes at both levels. Engaging in long-term, focused learning opportunities that blend theory, research, and practice will produce far greater results than listening to motivational speakers or attending a session to complete "in-service" requirements. As Schmoker (1999, 2006) believes and reflected in the titles for his books on school improvement, "results" are the bottom line. Mentoring new teachers and enhancing the capacities of their experienced colleagues is a means to achieve that end.

MOVING SCHOOL-BASED MENTORING PROGRAMS TO HIGHER LEVELS

Mentor Core Teams at each school should also think of their program in the same way (See figure 20.1). School-based mentoring and induction programs provide an opportune context for embedded professional development tailored to the specific needs of beginning and experienced teachers. We must accept that ours is a profession where we are continually refining our practice, setting higher goals for ourselves and our students, and modeling lifelong learning. How can we accomplish this effectively if we are not framing our decisions and plans on data and impact? Thinking about the quality of your program in impacting teaching and learning through the lens of Guskey's (2002) professional development model is a starting point. As you read this section, reflect on "what is" with your program—and "what ought to be" to move it forward most effectively to achieve your clearly articulated desired "results." Remember, you will revisit this information again and again as you grow your program—hopefully at Guskey's higher levels.

- **Level 1.** *Participants' reactions* have traditionally been the primary focus of this level of professional development. School leaders and Mentor Core Teams (first or second year) who are functioning at this level are most concerned with how teachers perceive the assignment of a mentor and the mentoring experiences that have been provided for them. The importance of these decisions is critical to keeping new teachers at the school and/or in the profession. Kozol (2007) credits "the best among them" in reference to talented experienced teachers who support new teachers as providing a "protective kindness that can be a salvatory comfort for a novice teacher under stress" (p. 40). While this is an acknowledged starting point, MCTs should strive to move up Guskey's steps to higher levels of impact where the emphasis transitions from teachers' satisfaction to teachers' capacity to produce desired teaching and learning outcomes.
- **Level 2.** At this level, *participants' learning,* MCTs plan for and monitor how the support provided is helping mentors and teachers become more effective educators who are capable of producing desired student outcomes. This requires that MCTs rethink the structure of the support that is being provided. For example, helping new teachers feel a sense of belonging is an admirable goal and may, in the long run, assure that they return to the school rather than request a transfer to a more collegial teaching environment. However, assuring that new teachers are effectively socialized may not impact their becoming more effective educators. As we know from both research and practice, teachers enter the profession to make a difference in students' lives and often leave when they perceive their working conditions and their own sense of efficacy as inhibiting their professional goal. MCTs that recognize the importance of helping new teachers become effective in their professional roles pay close attention to how their programs are structured. They want to assure a seamless transition from preservice to in-service teaching—and purposefully acclimate them to the teaching and learning expectations in their new school setting.
- **Level 3.** Addressing the challenge of *organizational support and change,* MCTs realize the teacher-mentoring program has implications for experienced teachers as well as those new to the profession or school. They expand their programs to involve

experienced teachers in sharing and learning with the beginning teachers and, in many of the schools with whom we have worked, become more integrally involved in the school's professional development. They begin to recognize what our partnering schools have termed "we don't know what we don't know." At this level, MCTs begin to inform school improvement based on their increased knowledge of what is working well and what needs to be strengthened in teacher mentoring.

• **Level 4.** At this level, *participants' use of new knowledge and skills*, MCTs are using assessment data to drive their programs. They want to assure that the professional development and support being provided for new teachers, mentoring colleagues, and school faculty are making a difference in their classrooms. Many provide additional training in teacher peer coaching (e.g., cognitive coaching) to assure that mentors have the knowledge and skills to coach effectively. They are more likely to be sharing ideas and strategies across the school to assure that teaching is improving in all classrooms—even those of experienced teachers who are beginning to realize the power of embedded professional development.

• **Level 5.** At Guskey's (2002) highest level, *student outcomes*, MCTs realize that unless what they are doing is having a direct impact on student learning, they are not accomplishing all that they can. This is where the transformational leadership of highly effective MCTs emerges. Effective schools recognize that school improvement planning must highlight the importance of having talented teachers in every classroom and of new teacher mentoring as a tool for attracting and retaining talented new teachers. At this level, teachers and administrators are using student data to inform their mentor program refinements, the development of mentors, and the professional growth of new teachers and their colleagues. As a result, the school is permeated with a sense of collaboration, support, trust, and professionalism. This is the "higher level" to which our effective mentor programs have transitioned and the "gold standard" we envision for your schools.

**Figure 20.1   Mentoring as Collaboration:
Continuous Improvement Steps and Feedback Loop**

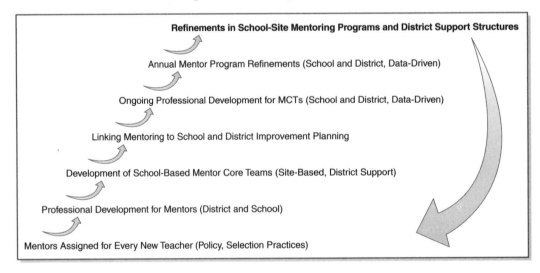

MOVING DISTRICT MENTORING PROGRAMS TO HIGHER LEVELS

When this model is translated to the district level, it becomes even more powerful. When school districts recognize the link between effective teachers and student achievement, they then rethink a number of policies, from the assignment of mentors to the placement of new teachers. For example, many school districts have been changing policies related to the hiring of new teachers and their placements in high-need schools, limiting extracurricular assignments, and providing additional "paid" professional development before school starts. In some school districts, an additional level of support is provided for new teachers in particularly high-need schools or classrooms, on either a voluntary or a required basis. The New Teacher Project at Santa Cruz model is one example of this external mentoring support provided at the district level. Training district supervisors in effective mentoring strategies provides additional support in many districts. Yet others are developing special professional development sessions and online support structures that add to the support provided at the school level.

Many school districts that have committed to supporting the professional growth of new teachers have also transformed professional development from the traditional smorgasbord approach to site-based, embedded peer coaching. They are training talented teachers in each school to assume a teacher leadership role in supporting beginning teachers. The district's role, then, becomes one of providing ongoing professional development to assure that Lead Mentors and Mentor Core Team members are well trained to carry out their roles at the school level. The most talented MCT members, who also have the knowledge and skills to serve as teacher trainers, often begin to assume even greater districtwide leadership roles—as teachers.

With these support structures in place, districts are also able to address the issue of teaching being a "flat career" where the only advancement opportunities are for teachers to leave the classrooms, where they are most effective, in order to move into administrative roles. Furthermore, when they monitor the impact of their systemic mentoring program, they begin to identify other professional development or organizational needs that might not have been apparent prior to collecting data on teacher retention, satisfaction, and student achievement gains.

Each school or district is at a different stage of organizational readiness for high levels of collaboration, distributed leadership, and shared responsibility. Likewise, each individual educator is at a different stage of maturity for being a productive professional in accepting high-level expectations and leadership responsibilities. The goal is to start where the people and organizational conditions are and grow to higher levels of professional learning and leadership. The ability of individuals and organizations to move to higher levels is influenced by many forces presenting some appealing opportunities as well as some challenges to overcome. According to Elmore (2000), "Learning to do the right thing—collectively, progressively, cumulatively over time" is a developmental process (p. 23). All educators,

> ❝ ———— **A Comment From the Field** ————
>
> Mentoring acts as a catalyst for veteran teachers to develop trust with other educators and comfort in sharing their ideas and experiences. This enables them to grow professionally, thus improving the education for students throughout schools and districts. What almost all mentors will say is that the benefits are to the givers as well as to the receivers.
>
> *Instructional Supervisor*
> ❞

even those in "relatively high-performing schools and districts," need to expand their focus beyond just improving practice to teaching people in the organization "how to think and act around learning for continuous improvement" (p. 31).

Our experience has shown that schools and districts that support highly effective teacher leaders and a culture of distributed or shared leadership can significantly improve student learning (Kershaw et al., 2006). Why? Schools with strong teacher leadership, led by Mentor Core Teams, have found ways to build the capacity of experienced teachers to support beginning teachers, design and facilitate professional development for their new and veteran colleagues, participate in hiring new teachers and supporting their growth, collaborate with colleagues, serve as *critical friends* in observing peers and sharing student or teacher work, and coach with research-based recommendations. The new teachers who are mentored into the profession in a collaborative culture have had firsthand experiences with these practices and will be more capable of and committed to replicating them throughout their careers. Having experienced the modeling of professional educators (veteran teachers and administrators) using reflection and problem solving to promote efficacy, beginning teachers will be better prepared to approach their careers with a sense of responsibility and internal standards of accountability that reflect what has been exhibited by their professional colleagues. As they follow their models and exhibit efficacy in creating relationships with their own students and their families, they become role models for those who follow them.

Educators in schools and districts with effective mentor programs also have opportunities to build their own capacities to achieve their desired outcomes. Leaders at both levels recognize the need to create organizational conditions that promote growth. Many leaders heed Elmore's (2000) recommendation for educator transformation: "frame their responsibilities in terms of their contribution to enhancing someone else's capacity and performance" (p. 32). Leadership capacity and professional growth can be promoted when administrators and teacher leaders routinely engage in observation and reflection on practice in schools and classrooms; master ways of talking about practice that allow for nonthreatening support, criticism, and judgment; and, most important, confront isolation.

✔ **Research to Practice Insight:** It has been our experience that districts grow their programs on a school-by-school basis. When district leaders become aware of the benefits school-based mentor teams produce, they develop confidence in the model and then want to expand it to all schools. In addition, significant impact comes from districts adopting mentoring policies and structures that provide guidance and support to schools in designing their own programs. Clearly defined goals, performance benchmarks, and adequate resources, combined with the flexibility to tailor the program to each school's unique context, are the keys to successful program implementation.

One major challenge faced by schools and districts is to make the fundamental changes that sustain continuous improvement. Changing the norms that shape how educators think about their work and how they will work together to raise the bar for their teaching and student learning requires leadership committed to systemic reform. We believe that collaborative teacher mentoring, at its highest level, provides a model that has the potential to transform schools and districts into the real communities of learning that Elmore (2000) describes.

Resource A

Observation Guidelines and Strategies

Purpose: To ensure that observations are positive, productive experiences for both parties

Timing: Throughout the year, whenever observations are conducted

1. *Confer with your protégé to determine the best times to observe and the best location for the observer.* It might be helpful to have a seating chart and any handouts for students.

2. *Be in place before the designated observation time.* This will avoid causing any disruption to the teacher's schedule or the class in general.

3. *Stay throughout an instructional segment.* See how it is introduced, implemented, and closed.

4. *Be unobtrusive.* Do not interact with students or the teacher during the observation. If the teacher asks a question, answer as quickly as possible and resume your role.

5. *Sit as close to the side of the classroom as possible.* This provides the best view of what is taking place and does not divert students' attention away from the teacher.

6. *Be sure you have a watch or clock in view.* This is essential if you are noting the length of the lesson segments, transitions, and events. Also, be sure to have additional materials on hand (e.g., extra paper, pens, pencils).

66 —— **A Comment From the Field** ——

Many of our veteran faculty have the traditional view of being observed—stress! We want to change the mindset about colleague or administrator observations from anxiety and trepidation to comfort and appreciation. We want frequent observations to become just "the way we do business." As mentor coaches, we've tried to find ways to alleviate any stress about having another adult in the room. We've found that asking our protégés to observe us first is a good way to start the process. We also ask the new teachers to tell us when the best time is to observe. On the first observation, we'll suggest that we focus on the kids or look at the room arrangement as a nonthreatening approach. Our protégés tell us that they appreciate having "another pair of eyes" to see what's going on. Observations have been rewarding experiences for both parties—we both learn so many techniques that translate into better teaching.

Mentor in a Large Intermediate School

99

7. *Give your notes to the new teacher after they have been used in the coaching session.* DO NOT share observation notes or impressions with others (administrator, colleagues).

OBSERVATIONAL STRATEGIES

- **Note times:** Throughout the lesson, record the time when important events, actions, and statements occur. This information aids in giving feedback related to the overall lesson and pacing. Note these events with anecdotal descriptions such as those listed below.
    - o An **important event** occurs during the lesson—with anecdotal descriptions such as bell rings (or, if there is no bell, the time that the lesson begins), beginning and other structuring statements, late student enters, transition signals to move from one major topic or activity to another, significant deviation from the learning focus, interruption to the lesson, beginning and ending of activity segments.
    - o A **significant action** takes place—student appropriate behaviors or misbehaviors, preventive or reactive disciplinary actions.
    - o A **notable teacher or student statement** is made—a comment or a question.
- **Identify participants:** Develop symbols or notations that work for your situation.

    T Teacher   O **Female Student**   □ **Male Student**

- **Create a drawing or map of the instructional setting (whole classroom or small group) to**
    - o identify teachers' questioning patterns (levels of questions, to whom they are directed);
    - o identify which students are responding to questions and how accurately they are answered; and
    - o track the physical movement of the teacher or students (obtaining materials, demonstrations, monitoring students working independently or in groups)
- **Provide descriptions of classroom events.** Describe classroom events objectively—just the facts—times and what is taking place.

Classroom Events				
Whole group teacher-led activity	**Independent work**	**Students working in pairs or groups**	**Management Tasks, Routines, Transitions**	**Teacher Actions or Statements**
• Lecture • Presentation • Direct instruction • Recitation • Discussion • Technology demonstration • Other, specify:	• From text • From workbook or activity page • Test or quiz • Using technology • Reading a book • Learning center (or computer-based activity) • Other, specify:	• Lab exercises • Tutoring • Creating a product • Cooperative learning team activity • Questioning strategies that pair students • Teacher-led small groups (other students engaged in other ways)	• Checking roll • Handing out papers • Responding to a message from the office or late student entry to class • Structure for moving from one lesson segment to another • Instructions identified on board or wall • Transitioning students to cooperative learning teams	• Structuring the class session • Giving directions • Introducing a topic • Describing the organization of the materials being handed out • Relating information to previous topics • Presenting information • Defining words • Giving examples • Using analogies • Illustrating ideas • Reviewing a topic • Summarizing • Reteaching • Pointing out a problem • Reminding students • Giving homework assignments

Using anecdotal statements. Observers who are focusing on teacher verbal statements often switch to anecdotal logs when teachers interrupt the verbal interaction to give students an opportunity to practice skills being taught or when they give students independent or small group assignments. When using anecdotal logs

- **Describe small-group work**
  - o student roles in small groups
  - o student movement among centers, lab areas, or other designated places
  - o teacher response to groups or individual students with questions
  - o teacher monitoring

- **Describe how students are engaged.**
  - o All students are doing the same instructional activity
  - o All students (individuals and groups) are involved in various instructional activities
  - o Some students are engaged in activities that do not appear to be instructional
  - o Many students are engaged in activities that do not appear to be instructional
  - o (All, some, many students) Brief transition time before reengaging in learning activities

- **Note the use of research-based or advocated instructional strategies.**
  - o Essential Questions (posted and/or incorporated)
  - o Rubrics (use of or evidence of)
  - o Graphic Organizers or Thinking Maps (use of or evidence of)
  - o Literacy Development
    - Writing activity (or evidence of—recent student work displayed)
    - Vocabulary (or Concept) develop or Word Block activity
    - Independent Reading (use of leveled libraries, Teacher-Student conferences, other)
    - Guided Reading activities (teaching or using reading strategies)
  - o Teaching a skill (procedural knowledge or other skill including a higher-level thinking skill)
    - Clear steps to follow
    - Visuals to reinforce verbal instructions
    - Time provided for students to practice
  - o Teaching a concept
    - Linking the new concept to students' prior knowledge
    - Providing students with cues for remembering the new concept
    - Helping students organize what they are learning (notes, graphics)

- **Develop a strategy for recording verbal statements and interactions.** When an observer limits the focus to teacher questions and actions, it is possible to write out each question asked. Rather than writing out student responses, indicate the correctness of the student answer after each question. When students ask questions or make comments, you can also code them without writing out exactly what is said.

Recording students' verbal statements and questions			
Coding student responses to teacher questions or structuring statements		**Coding student questions and comments**	
+	Correct answers	S?	• Student asks a question
+/–	Partially correct answers	S?s	• Students asking questions at one time
–	Incorrect answers		
SV	Student volunteers to respond	S?c	• Student asks a content-related question
NV	Teacher calls on student to respond (not a volunteer)		
XR	Student extended reply	S?p	• Student asks a procedural question
CR	Choral response		
VCOR	Various called out responses	SC	• Student comment
RH	Student's hand is raised	SCc	• Student comment – content related
RR	Student refuses request		
////	Wait time (one one-thousand, two one-thousand)	SCp	• Student comment – procedural
TP	Teacher probes for an answer		
TC	Teacher cue		

Notes:

- To capture a questioning strategy that involves an initial incorrect or partially correct answer that the teacher wants the student to improve, you can use a series of codes. Try to capture the teacher questions, but if you cannot (rapid pace), do the following:

  Why do you think that . . . ? SR-/TP/SR+

- When students are interacting with one another, use the following to code the interactions:
  - S-S   Student responds/talks to another student or students
  - SS-SS   Many students responding/talking to other students

Resource B

*Research-Based Actions and/or
Recommendations Linked to INTASC Standards*

Purpose: To improve new teacher's instructional practice by providing research-based recommendations and strategies that will assist beginning teachers in meeting the expectations of professional standards and principles.

Timing: During consultations, formal and informal conferences, and when modeling "Best Practices," observing instruction and giving feedback, planning collaboratively with your protégé, strategizing for school improvement, analyzing student data analysis throughout the induction period.

INTASC is the Interstate New Teacher Assessment & Support Consortium and is the work of A Program of the Council of Chief State School Officers. Their *Model Standards for Beginning Teacher Licensing, Assessment and Development: A Resource for State Dialogue* (1992) outlines the knowledge, dispositions, and performances deemed essential for all teachers regardless of the subject or grade level being taught. Drafted by a committee of teachers, teacher educators, and state agency officials, they represent a shared view of what constitutes competent beginning teaching. The INTASC principles are currently being expanded for various subject matter areas and specific student populations. This resource provides INTASC principles followed by a list of specific strategies, gleaned from both research and practice, to use in helping new teachers succeed in addressing the INTASC expectations.

PRINCIPLE 1: SUBJECT MATTER

The teacher understands the central concepts, tools of inquiry, and structures of the discipline(s) he or she teaches and can create learning experiences that make these aspects of subject matter meaningful for students.

Identify supplementary resources to strengthen knowledge of the subject to ensure accuracy.

- Guide in identifying important concepts, skills, and enduring understandings.
- Guide in finding additional resource materials and in developing instructional strategies that will engage the students in meaningful learning experiences that apply knowledge and skills in real world contexts.

Point out subject-specific academic vocabulary students should acquire.

- Point out important ways the content is used by the experts in the field, the "real world" work they do, their contributions, and their roles.
- Point out examples to incorporate in instruction and assessments.

Point out the typical misconceptions students may have related to content or skills.

- Guide in developing formal and informal strategies for assessing students' pre-instructional understanding so that misconceptions are corrected and accurate understandings are reinforced.

Identify important discipline-specific methods and instructional strategies.

- Suggest specific readings, resources, and professional development opportunities to gain tools of inquiry and content-related structures.

Guide in planning logical, coherent presentations that build on previously mastered content and connect to future content or skills.

- Structure of content should be conveyed clearly to students incorporating effective visual and/or verbal advance organizers to provide an overview of the content.

Model the processes for organizing content and double checking for accuracy.

- Identify ways to emphasize important points, summarize, and review.
- Incorporate relevant and fascinating stories, examples, and/or analogies to enhance students' acquisition of content that boost interest and energy!

Point out connections to concepts and skills taught in one subject to other subjects.

- Identify opportunities to appropriately integrate content from different disciplines to help students make meaningful connections.
- Link new teachers with other faculty who can help them make these content area connections.

Identify strategies, questions, and tasks that engage students in higher level learning challenges.

- Emphasize that all students need opportunities to extend and refine their knowledge.
- Share strategies that encourage students to see, question, and interpret ideas from diverse perspectives.
- Prompt reflection about evidence of students' higher level thinking.

Model a process for evaluating teaching resources and curriculum materials.

- Point out the appropriateness to students' needs as well as accuracy and usefulness for representing particular ideas and concepts.

PRINCIPLE 2: STUDENT LEARNING

The teacher understands how children and youth learn and develop, and can provide learning opportunities that support their intellectual, social, and personal growth.

Share preassessments that identify what students already know and can do, then model how to build on strengths.
- Share formal and informal assessment strategies for systematically gathering accurate and adequate background information about students' needs in each domain (cognitive, social, emotional, moral, and physical) and using the information to plan instruction.
- Share samples of interest inventories, learning style/MI assessments, etc., so that individual and collective assets of students are identified and used in planning.
- Suggest learning experiences (including readings, videos, vocabulary, and activities) that could give students the needed background knowledge so that they have some familiar knowledge on which to build.

Model a process for analyzing student performance data.
- Use aggregated and disaggregated data from state and classroom assessments to identify the diverse needs of students as a whole class, as groups, and as individuals.

Ask questions to prompt reflection about the whole child—their physical, social, emotional, moral, and cognitive development.
- Point out readiness levels, expected developmental progressions, and ranges of individual variation within each domain and strategies to promote student growth (physical, social, emotional, moral, and cognitive).
- Provide guidance in creating a classroom learning community where individual differences are respected and positive relationships are evident.
- Point out ways to adapt practices to be consistent with students' level of self-discipline and need for structure.

Model respect for the diverse talents, interests, and perspectives of all learners and a commitment to helping each student develop self-confidence and competence.
- Share age-appropriate strategies that promote students' ownership of the learning.
- Model actions and language that reflect the belief that *all* children can learn at high levels.
- Model problem solving and persistence in helping all children strengthen their efforts to achieve their "personal bests."
- Emphasize the importance of knowing and following regulations about confidentiality of information.

Provide guidance to align classroom management practices with students' academic, personal, and social needs.
- Point out ways to adapt practices to be consistent with students' level of self-discipline and need for structure.

Discuss important "Habits of Mind" (Marzano et al., 2001) or dispositions toward learning.
- Share specific *life skills* that are important to incorporate in everyday instruction and interactions.
- Discuss how they can be included in assignments, rubrics, formal, and informal feedback. One example is to model how to value student errors as opportunities for learning.

PRINCIPLE 3: DIVERSE LEARNERS

The teacher understands how students differ in their approaches to learning and creates instructional opportunities that are adapted to learners from diverse cultural backgrounds and to those with exceptionalities.

Point out resources with information about areas of exceptionality (e.g., learning disabilities, visual and perceptual difficulties, special physical or mental challenges, and gifted and talented).

- Collaborate to identify appropriate instructional adaptations to meet the needs of learners with specific exceptionalities.
- Make information available about service providers and the procedures for accessing appropriate resources to meet exceptional learning needs.

Model how to plan to meet the learning needs of individuals and groups.

- Ensure an understanding of students' IEP and collaboration with special educators to ensure that IEPs are being correctly implemented to the fullest extent possible.

Point out resources with information about how second language is acquired.

- Share and model research-based practices that support ELL students.
- Model collaboration with ELL teachers in identifying instructional adaptations to meet the specific needs of ELL students.

Share resources and model plans that incorporate multicultural issues and content (i.e., the language as well as family and community values, people within the community, community resources, cultural events, places, and concerns).

- Provide guidance in developing culturally and contextually relevant instruction that incorporates student's experiences, cultures, and community resources and how to include multiple perspectives in discussions.
- Identify timely, relevant issues or problems of interest to students.
- Identify positive role models, examples, and illustrations from more than one culture.
- Engage in Community Mapping, take a community tour, or introduce new teachers to a community mentor.

Model respectful interactions with students and with parenting adults of various backgrounds.

- Point out specifically how to show sensitivity to individuals and community or cultural norms. Highlight important actions, language, and contextual considerations.
- Share your rationale and professional thinking and provide information (articles, books) to stimulate thinking about how to work with students from cultures other than their own.

Share model plans for differentiated content assignments for students.

- Point out how specific structures, strategies, activities, and assessments are adjusted.
- Identify specific reading strategies to help students with reading difficulties.
- Identify modifications and accommodations for special needs students (remediation or alternative approaches for the slower students as well as acceleration or challenge activities for the more able students).
- Point out ways to adjust time and circumstances for work, tasks assigned, communication, and response modes.
- Identify appropriate alternatives to address different MI or learning styles.

PRINCIPLE 4: INSTRUCTIONAL STRATEGIES

The teacher understands and uses a variety of instructional strategies to encourage students' development of critical thinking, problem solving, and performance skills.

Discuss what teachers acting as facilitators of learning do and say.
- Show how to vary the instructional role, task structure, mode of instruction, or grouping of students within the learning period to more appropriately meet student needs.
- Point out appropriate points in lessons to incorporate the use of cooperative learning, independent learning, and/or learning centers.
- Describe or demonstrate strategies for facilitating efficient transitions between instructional segments.

Point out when opportunities for developing students' critical and creative thinking and problem solving can be incorporated.
- Emphasize thinking and model the language of thinking.
- Provide strategies for explicit instruction in the steps of higher-level thinking processes (i.e., comparison, classifying, induction, deduction, and abstracting).
- Model a "Think-Aloud" process to highlight teacher thinking.
- Point out opportunities when students can apply higher-level thinking in meaningful ways—so that application is automatic, independent, and transferred to other contexts.

Recommend the use of inquiry and discovery techniques.
- Share ways to be responsive to student thinking and reasoning to help students integrate new information with prior knowledge.
- Identify opportunities for creating data; make observations; interpret data to make predictions and draw conclusions; form hypotheses; manipulate objects; present data on grids; tables, etc.

Emphasize the connection between various instructional models and their specific learning purposes.
- Point out when direct instruction is recommended.
- Identify additional models (e.g. concept attainment, inquiry, debate, project-based, problem-based) for other purposes and content areas.

Provide support for the use of differentiated instructional strategies.
- Point out when learning centers, learning stations, tiered activities, contracts, etc. are effective in meeting students' varied learning styles and needs.
- Identify strategies to use to organize and monitor differentiated, independent, and group work that will allow for full and varied participation of all students.

Point out opportunities to incorporate peer interaction and cooperative learning.
- Collaborate on the needed structure to ensure that the interactions lead to higher-level learning and new levels of understanding and improved comprehension.

Point out opportunities to integrate technology.
- Model ways to use technology that require students to explore, respond, and extend their thinking.
- Share strategies for the efficient use of technology in the classroom and in technology labs.

Point out techniques to facilitate productive classroom discussion.
- Provide a model for developing a questioning strategy and effective questioning techniques.
- Talk about ways to incorporate appropriate wait time with higher-level questions.
- Point out ways to manage response opportunities to include all students and use appropriate reactions (i.e., probing, redirecting, feedback, and wait time) to improve the quality of student thinking.
- Model how to encourage student comments and questions that develop the content and promote student understanding.
- Share strategies to promote student thinking and risk taking, such as identifying questions for which there are no wrong answers and situations with several possible solutions or leading students to ask questions and/or pose meaningful problems.

Model how to develop clear explanations of concepts.
- Identify essential facts and concepts (declarative knowledge) and strategies for learning them.
- Collaborate to develop multiple representations and explanations of the content to assure students' understanding.
- Show how to carefully choose definitions, examples, and explanations to enhance student understanding of concepts.
- Show ways to incorporate structuring statements to enhance clarity.
- Design specific dates to incorporate systematic review (about every 20 days) to ensure retention of essential concepts.
- Use mnemonic devices, imagery strategies, or graphic organizers to help input information in ways that make retrieval easier.

Identify strategies to activate students' prior knowledge.
- Model how to incorporate approaches to build on or extend accurate knowledge (linking new knowledge to familiar concepts) or confront inaccurate knowledge (teaching for conceptual change).
- Identify effective vocabulary acquisition strategies to incorporate.

Model the steps for teaching procedures, skills, or processes.
- Identify essential procedural skills and develop appropriate schedules to help studetns shape and internalize them.
- Point out ways to scaffold students' learning by providing cognitive organizers, visual cues, and other resources.
- Identify an appropriate review cycle (about every 20 days for essential procedures) so that students maintain their proficiency.
- Share practice strategies and application or extension opportunities.

Identify the essential declarative and procedural knowledge and plan adequate and appropriately spaced opportunities for review and practice.
- Designate specific dates to incorporate systematic review (about every 20 days) to ensure retention of essential concepts and skills.

Share techniques to clarify directions and explanations to avoid student frustration.
- Provide ways to elaborate explanations so that students have a clear understanding.
- Model Me (teacher think-aloud)-We (guided practice)-Two (partners)-You (independent application) [as recommended by Modern Red Schoolhouse].

- Suggest checking with target students to assess their level of understanding and the need to provide additional explanations.

Develop and rehearse alternative explanations of important concepts.
- Plan explanations that link to several multiple intelligences.
- Incorporate multisensory experiences, use graphic organizers, manipulatives, and concrete or "hands on" learning.

Collaborate to identify appropriate pacing of lessons to meet students' needs.
- Point out the challenges that result from inappropriate pacing (i.e., if pace is too rapid, students do not understand and don't complete assignments; if pace is uneven, students do not have ample time to process all topics; and if pace is too slow, boredom and disengagement occur).

Show how to pace lessons based on student understanding.
- Guide in identifying target groups/students and pace instruction appropriately.
- Advise about staying focused on major topics, providing only appropriate explanatory information (irrelevant topics take valuable teaching time).
- Help to identify key indicators of student understanding to guide interactive decisions about the pace of the lesson.
- Identify points to incorporate frequent checks for student understanding and timely corrective feedback to correct misunderstanding.
- Point out optional structures for the point in the lesson when the majority of the students understand the instruction (e.g., independent, group work, or centers for most students while the teacher works with those who need additional assistance).

Share specific summarizing strategies to help students construct meaning.
- Point out times to incorporate large group, small group, and independent opportunities for students to process and integrate new learning with prior learning.
- Discuss the importance of providing specific and timely corrective feedback related to the task.
- Model techniques for giving feedback and identify a variety of ways to incorporate feedback.
- Provide strategies for overtly teaching summarizing strategies—a key to understanding main ideas and supporting details.

Provide advice on how to keep all students actively engaged.
- Implement specific strategies designed to increase students' motivation to learn.
- Incorporate "hands on, minds on" activities.
- Use graphic organizers to make learning more visual.
- Incorporate appropriate technology-based instructional resources.
- Redesign learning centers to reduce the amount of down time for students.
- Capitalize on student interest with "teachable moments."

Model techniques for monitoring and adjusting instruction.
- Discuss the importance of remaining alert to student attention, understanding, and behavior and of being flexible in making adjustments.
- Talk about possible interactive decisions to change instruction when situations warrant.
- Guide in planning for alternatives (*Plan B*), identifying relevant "time fillers" that require little or no additional planning.
- Model how to plan for and monitor longer-term individual or cooperative projects.

Identify strategies to promote students' responsibility for learning.
- Point out opportunities to incorporate goal setting, planning, and monitoring progress to increase students' self-regulated thinking.
- Model how to teach students learning strategies (e.g., determining main idea, reading visual information, summarizing, and reviewing).
- Discuss how to help students acquire strategies so that they own "tools" for learning future content.
- Identify how the strategies can be used in other content or aspects of students' lives.

PRINCIPLE 5: LEARNING ENVIRONMENT

The teacher uses an understanding of individual and group motivation and behavior to create a learning environment that encourages positive social interaction, active engagement in learning, and self-motivation.

Model professional responsibility for maintaining a positive classroom (and schoolwide) climate.
- Share and discuss schoolwide management plans, rules, consequences, and incentives to ensure consistent implementation in classrooms.

Collaborate to develop strategies that promote positive relationships, cooperation, and purposeful learning in the classroom.
- Suggest ways to ensure an emotionally safe and orderly classroom culture—one that values cooperation and respect for individual differences.
- Share a collaborative, democratic process for developing shared classroom rules with students.
- Identify specific strategies to help students develop ownership for learning.

Discuss how to establish a learning environment that promotes openness, mutual respect, support, and inquiry.
- Discuss the importance of using courteous, supportive interpersonal behaviors with students.
- Model mutually respectful interactions, the use of positive reinforcement to support desired behaviors, and ways to communicate concern for students as individuals.
- Emphasize the need to never use sarcasm or ridicule.
- Discuss the importance of creating a learning centered classroom climate where mistakes and failures become learning opportunities—and students are not afraid to take academic risks.

Point out important ways to promote students' intrinsic motivation and positive attitudes toward learning.
- Share ways to discover factors that motivate students and prompt their eagerness to learn.
- Guide in developing strategies that help students become self-motivated (intrinsic motivation).
- Model techniques for linking new learning to student interests and experiences and for providing students choice (equally acceptable options).

- Guide in understanding the effects of extrinsic rewards on students' motivation toward learning.
- Discuss how to use praise and reinforcement effectively.

Collaborate on important instructional routines to reduce managerial demands and distractions and to maintain an orderly, predictable flow of classroom events.

- Emphasize the need to be flexible when unexpected situations require reorganization or modification of classroom procedures.
- Emphasize the need to be ready for instruction; stay on task; avoid late starts or early endings; and maintain the academic focus.
- Develop routines for checking attendance, handing out or collecting papers, moving to centers, learning stations, or labs, and other daily tasks.
- Identify quick, "no planning required," interactive activities to use with students to avoid wasted down time.
- Guide in identifying a range of appropriate opening or "warm up" activities.
- Share how to provide students with clear guidelines for completing class work and homework, especially when the assignment(s) call for higher-order thinking.

Provide suggestions for organizing and arranging the classroom.

- Recommend ways to help students "own" their classroom, such as locations to display student work.
- Discuss the need for efficient monitoring and noncongested student movement.
- Suggest places for materials and equipment that allow for easy access and for visual monitoring.
- Identify needed areas for instructional purposes, for management, and for temporary and more permanent storage.
- Suggest visiting other teachers' classrooms to identify additional helpful ideas.

Share strategies for managing classroom resources effectively.

- Share beginning-of-the-year procedures to promote comfort in the environment.
- Guide in developing rules, procedures, and consequences (positive and negative).
- Talk about how to clearly communicate behavioral expectations and how to monitor for compliance.
- Emphasize the need to follow through consistently on consequences.
- Focus attention on how to ensure active and equitable engagement of students in productive tasks.
- Develop effective procedures for students who were absent (e.g., handling makeup work, connecting students to the work they missed, learning partners or teams, agendas, checklists of expectations, video- or audio-taped instruction, notes, handouts, alternative assignments, small group catch-up sessions, etc.).

Model smooth, efficient transitions and ways to reengage learners.

- Talk about how to gain and keep students' attention.
- Guide in developing structuring statements and signals for transition times to promote faster reengagement.
- Practice ways to communicate what students are expected to do as well as what they are expected to learn during the activity.
- Stress the importance of actively monitoring student engagement (e.g., how to circulate purposefully, intervene, provide feedback, and hold students individually accountable).

Point out how to direct and manage cooperative work.

- Model how to communicate specific expectations for student participation including assignment of roles, time frames, ways to get assistance, etc.
- Point out opportunities for students to develop leadership and responsibility.
- Talk about how to teach social skills and how to monitor for their appropriate use.

Share strategies to help students develop self-regulated behaviors.

- Point out how to teach self-regulated learning (e.g., being aware of own thinking, planning their work, working their plan, evaluating actions).
- Guide in identifying incentives to encourage appropriate behavior.
- Point out opportunities for students to monitor their own learning and to set goals for improvement.
- Share guidelines about setting challenging, attainable, rigorous goals and ways to encourage commitment, such as allowing some flexibility and individuality in determining how they will meet their goals.

Discuss appropriate corrective actions for inappropriate behavior.

- Point out acceptable corrective actions (e.g., school sanctioned, reasonable, fair, and linked logically to the misbehavior; use of problem-solving or conflict resolution processes).
- Emphasize the importance of intervening promptly, objectively, with as little disruption to the academic focus as possible.
- Discuss how to use corrective actions in constructive ways so that disruptions are resolved productively and classroom order is restored.
- Help develop skills in using constructive strategies to de-escalate potential conflicts.
- Suggest the use of formal class meetings to assess progress and set improvement goals.

Prompt reflection and problem solving on *ineffective* preventive classroom management practices (i.e., dealing with disruptive student behavior, a lack of respect for adults and for their peers).

- Guide in redesigning the management system to ensure appropriate learning behaviors and to correct inappropriate behavior.
- Identify several specific actions that can be taken to strengthen the personal relationship between the teacher and students (all or targeted students).
- Identify ways to strengthen and vary instructional activities to facilitate student learning and engagement.

Provide guidance in working with paraprofessionals or teaching assistants.

- Talk about specific work expectations, schedules, and additional commitments of the assistants.
- Share your tips about how you establish and maintain positive working relationships with other adults (routines, schedules, times set aside for planning meetings).

PRINCIPLE 6: COMMUNICATION

The teacher uses knowledge of effective verbal, nonverbal, and media communication techniques to foster active inquiry, collaboration, and supportive interaction in the classroom.

Model clear, proper, and appropriate communications with students, parents, and others.

- Point out verbal and nonverbal ways to demonstrate sensitivity to cultural and gender differences (e.g., use of eye contact, body language, word choice, pace, and volume).
- Guide reflection about the effects of communication and response related to cultural dynamics.
- Emphasize the need to use appropriate grammar, logical organization of information, word choice, and vocabulary that reflects knowledge of the content and the audience.
- Assure that new teachers understand that all written communication should be carefully proofread before sending to colleagues, parents, or persons outside the school.
- Emphasize the need to avoid educational jargon when communicating to parents.
- Emphasize the need to avoid sarcasm in any professional communication—especially with students.
- Model being a thoughtful and responsive listener and ways to provide reinforcement for appropriate listening behaviors.

Guide reflection on effective nonverbal communications.

- Point out key nonverbal behaviors that enhance communication and set goals to incorporate.
- Suggest videotaping and collegial analysis of the taped interactions, paying attention to instances of misaligned nonverbal behaviors with the verbal message, or to inappropriate or ineffective communications.

Provide feedback if inappropriate or incorrect grammar is used in oral or written communications.

- Offer assistance in proofing written communications (to adults, to students) for accurate spelling, sentence construction, and organization of content.
- Identify ways to monitor speech patterns to reflect proper grammatical usage.
- Suggest audiotaping, collegial analysis, and identify goals for growth.

Collaborate to develop effective questioning strategies.

- Guide in planning questions above the recall level of thinking. Refer to Bloom's Taxonomy (1981) or Marzano et al.'s *Dimensions of Learning* (1997) for specific strategies to develop appropriate content questions that require higher-level thinking.
- Help develop verbal and/or visual techniques appropriate for probing, prompting, and cueing to help students improve their responses; promoting risk-taking; encouraging convergent and divergent thinking; stimulating curiosity; and prompting students to question.
- Discuss the importance of stimulating students' critical thinking by asking "Why?" and "What is your evidence?"
- Develop strategies for assuring that all students have an opportunity to answer questions (i.e., chalk or white boards at students' desks, cards with students' names, think-pair-share, numbered heads together).

- Identify opportunities to engage students in structured debate, dramatic activities, simulations, or creative representations in which they are engaged in answering higher-order questions or solving complex problems.
- Help develop strategies for involving students in asking higher-order questions—a well documented technique for improving performance in answering them.

Share communication strategies that expand learners' expression in speaking, writing, and other media.

- Guide in planning lessons that engage students in cooperative work where they must take and defend a position to address a question or problem posed by the teacher.
- Help design peer writing (i.e., prewriting, writing, editing) experiences when appropriate.
- Help design group problem- or project-based learning activities that engage students in writing scripts or documents, sharing them with their classmates, and using media as part of their presentation.
- Guide in developing independent student projects that incorporate problem- or project-based learning, writing, speaking, and use of media.
- Share rubrics for speaking, writing, and the use of media.
- Plan implementation strategies when introducing and using rubrics.

Discuss the importance of teacher enthusiasm.

- Model statements that convey enthusiasm and positive dispositions for learning and the content.
- Talk about elements of enthusiasm in delivery (vary voice level, use nonverbal gestures, move about the room).
- Suggest videotaping and collegial analysis focused on indicators of enthusiasm.

Emphasize the importance of communicating success expectations to students.

- Model ways to communicate the belief that *ALL* students can learn.
- Guide in developing statements that convey success expectations for all students. "You can do it" is one of the most powerful statements teachers make. Teachers then must provide the right instructional conditions to make success (or improvement) possible for each student.
- Help students understand and celebrate their own progress (i.e., charts, tracking grades, setting goals, and monitoring progress).
- Guide in providing credible, specific, and age-appropriate praise and reinforcement to acknowledge effort, progress, and/or achievement.
- Identify points and processes for praise and reinforcement to be incorporated.

Model effective media communication techniques that incorporate a variety of communication modes.

- Guide in developing skills using a variety of media communication tools.
- Collaborate on planning to incorporate communication tools in lessons.

Discuss the need to communicate with parenting adults and others on a frequent, timely, and regular basis.

- Share techniques to communicate in multiple ways and on a timely and frequent basis.
- Guide in making initial contacts with families at the beginning of the year or semester. Share the importance of establishing relationships prior to having to discuss any instructional or behavioral problems.

- Share approved processes for communicating progress to students and others, including teacher Web sites as well as sample letters, notes, newsletters, etc.
- Share how curriculum expectations are communicated to parents.
- Share strategies for positive meetings with parents (e.g., open houses, parent conferences).

PRINCIPLE 7: PLANNING INSTRUCTION

The teacher plans and manages instruction based upon knowledge of subject matter, students, the community, and curriculum goals.

Share formats, requirements, and resources for daily and unit planning.

- Share current curriculum frameworks, maps, or pacing guides. [For K–8 teachers, it is especially important to have access to curriculum guides for grades above and grades below (including preschool). For secondary teachers, it is important to have access to curriculum expectations for prior or foundational courses and any courses that build on their course(s).]
- Share dates for school, department, grade-level, or classroom and instructionally related events such as open house, parent conferences, test days, breaks, etc.
- Guide in developing daily and weekly schedules, including instructional and noninstructional times.
- Help develop unit plans with meaningful lessons arranged in logical order to accomplish a specific purpose.
- Share sample lesson and unit plans—and show how to access others on state Web sites or on the Internet.
- Provide a sample Emergency Plan for Substitutes that focuses on enrichment and/or practice rather than on new learning and guide in developing a plan.

Provide a clear model for planning.

- Model the practice of "planning with the end in mind" (Wiggins & McTighe, 1998). Focus on a clear understanding of the desired learning outcomes (standards) as the starting point for planning lessons and units.
- Articulate "teacher-thinking" highlighting the planning steps to follow or considerations and the connections to students' developmental stages.
- Point out why specific instructional strategies are incorporated to address students' learning styles and needs.
- Point out why a variety of structures are incorporated (e.g., whole group instruction, partner learning, cooperative learning, and independent work).
- Provide a model for differentiating instruction by readiness, interests, or learning styles to meet the strengths and needs of individuals and student groups. Share models that incorporate differentiated instructional strategies such as cooperative learning, learning centers or stations, tiered activities, agendas, and contracts.

Assist in developing plans that include clear and/or specific learning expectations.

- Provide a model plan that illustrates a logical, clear, and appropriate connection between goals and objectives and the developmental characteristics of all students.
- Collaboratively analyze the curriculum to determine essential (or priority) knowledge and skills (and high stakes assessment items) that students need to acquire—eliminating those that are neither essential nor important.

- Collaborate on developing "Essential Questions" to convey learning expectations or purpose for learning to students.
- Provide tips about how to use "Essential Questions" (where to post, how students record, summarizing strategies for responding, etc.).

Model collaborative planning with grade-level or departmental colleagues.

- Model collaborative planning with special education, ESL teachers, media specialists, technology specialists, instructional assistants, etc., so that mutual expectations and communication needs are addressed.
- Facilitate collegial discussions among grade-level teachers or with school guidance counselors about alignment of objectives and students' needs and abilities.
- Set up visits to classrooms (grade level, above grade, and below grade) to focus on level of expectations.

Guide in adapting plans to ensure maximum student progress and motivation.

- Guide in planning for alternatives (Plan B) to meet students' needs (when some students may become disengaged).
- Guide reflection on instruction and its effects on students' learning and motivation.
- Share ways to elicit input from students about topics that would stimulate their interest and desire to learn.
- Point out opportunities for students to reflect on their learning and their progress as learners.

Model the process of long-range planning and curriculum pacing.

- Talk about the importance of daily plans at the beginning with increasing emphasis on longer-term planning as the year progresses.
- Advise that planning decisions (i.e., breadth, depth, and sequencing) are made using academic curriculum standards and assessment priorities—planning with the end in mind (Marzano, 1997).
- Model the process of using the school calendar, pacing guides, and last year's plans to identify the days *not* available for instruction, noting opportunities for individualized or small-group instruction as well as for tutoring and enrichment.

Share model plans related to the development of thinking processes.

- Guide in planning for direct instruction and/or application of higher-level thinking processes most appropriate to the content and students' needs.
- Identify practice opportunities to use higher-level thinking on a regular basis.
- Identify assessments that will provide important feedback to students about the development of thinking processes.
- Point out ways to incorporate higher-order questions on tests or in performance assessments.

Guide in identifying the *BIG* ideas or powerful concepts in content areas.

- Collaborate to develop a concept map showing the major topics, subtopics, and the relationships among them.
- Identify key vocabulary, examples, significant concepts, and important skills.
- Point out the connections of new learning to prior and future learning and to other content areas.

Guide in planning integrated instruction and inquiry across content areas.

- Share model lesson plans with connected subjects integrated rather than segregated. Guide in rearranging lessons to more appropriately link or integrate content across subject areas. At the secondary level, engage new teachers in working with colleagues in subject areas that facilitate integration.

- Discuss the importance of interdisciplinary or thematic planning as a way to provide appropriate cohesion of content across subjects, productive inquiry, and maximum use of instructional time.

Guide in planning instruction that is connected to students' lives.

- Point out important connections between learning expectations and real-life experiences and future careers.
- Identify ways to communicate a clear rationale for why students need to learn content and how it applies to everyday life outside of school.
- Identify relevant, meaningful activities that relate directly to accomplishing objectives (i.e., worth the time, energy, and resource; activities predicted to bring about desired learning) in every lesson and unit plan.

Ensure that plans incorporate research-based strategies appropriate to the content area.

- Point out "generic" research-based strategies with broad application (e.g., graphic organizers, vocabulary development, cooperative learning, higher-level learning).
- Point out research-based strategies related to students' needs and abilities, especially for English language and special needs learners.
- Guide the incorporation of appropriate experiences that incorporate background knowledge and build on students' prior experiences, interests, and familiar knowledge.
- Guide reflection on the use of active learning strategies to keep students engaged.

Guide to incorporate a variety of instructional materials and resources in plans.

- Talk about the need to avoid an overreliance on textbooks.
- Suggest a variety of appropriate primary sources as instructional materials.
- Suggest technology and other supplementary nontechnical resources (outside experts from school families and the community at large) available to enhance instruction. If unfamiliar equipment, technology, or programs are included, make arrangements for needed assistance.
- Suggest the use of digital pictures and other examples from the community to promote meaning for students.

PRINCIPLE 8: ASSESSMENT

The teacher understands and uses formal and informal assessment strategies to evaluate and ensure the continuous intellectual, social, and physical development of the learner.

Provide information about the adopted grading system.

- Talk about the sources for grades and the relative weights of the various sources (percent of the total grade).
- Discuss homework, makeup work, and extra credit policies and how they align with the grading system.
- Talk about how students' grades are impacted by effort and improvement.

Guide to incorporate a variety of student evaluations and assessments.

- Guide reflection about the range of opportunities for students to show what they know and can do.

- Talk about the range of cognitive and affective assessments that can accurately assess students' academic progress and their attitudes toward learning.
- Share end-of-year indicators, benchmarks, or accomplishments and model *backwards* planning to ensure connections on a short-term and long-term basis.
- Share student self-assessment techniques.

Model the use of assessment results in planning future instruction, regrouping students, and providing needed and timely individualized assistance.

- Share preassessment strategies that clearly identify students' entry level knowledge and baseline skills.
- Model a process of using assessment data to improve student performance (i.e., disaggregating student achievement data by performance level and studying the impact of teaching on the performance of students at each level).
- Show how to develop realistic, reasonable, and differentiated expectations for student learning based on assessment data.

Guide reflection about the effect of grading practices on students' learning and motivation.

- If a high percentage of students earn failing grades (i.e., do not care, do not work to potential, do not complete or attempt assignments), guide in reexamining planning and grading practices to identify possible causes of poor performance or motivation.
- Collaborate to identify specific strategies to overcome negative influences on learning and to encourage students' reasonable effort.
- Discuss the possibilities of improvement grading and/or effort grading as sources for student grades.
- Rehearse ways to communicate high expectations for student performance and ways to provide adequate assistance and support to help all students succeed.
- Guide in targeting one or two students with potential for increased effort and developing motivational strategies to implement with these students. Study the impact of the strategies on the students' performance.

Discuss how to maintain useful records of student work and performance in order to communicate progress knowledgeably and responsibly.

- Stress the need to maintain accurate records of student progress.
- Guide in developing a grading system that incorporates a range of indicators of progress.
- Guide in developing a reporting system with timely notification to students and parenting adults.

Guide in developing a variety of ongoing assessments to monitor and promote student learning.

- Share academic (content- and skill-related) assessments used for diagnostic and placement purposes. Point out the purpose of the assessments, how the results are used, and any limitations.
- Model the use of a variety of formal and informal assessment techniques that provide accurate and adequate information about student progress (e.g. preassessments, summarizers, teacher observations, portfolios of student work, teacher-made tests, performance tasks, projects, student self-assessments, peer assessment, and standardized tests).

- Model the use of appropriate alternative assessments that require students to apply their knowledge in authentic ways as they would in the real world. Use supplements to traditional paper/pencil tests.

Guide in developing assessment strategies aligned with instructional objectives and standardized performance indicators.

- Guide in selecting, constructing, and using assessment strategies and instruments aligned with instruction and appropriate to the learning outcomes.
- Incorporate standardized test-like practice so students can experience the format and testing conditions.
- Use the practice as opportunities to develop confidence and test-taking skills.

Model the process of data analysis to identify student strengths and to promote growth.

- Collaboratively analyze assessment results to identify knowledge of learners, evaluate student's progress and performances, and modify teaching and learning strategies.
- Discuss how to use students' previous standardized test results to focus instruction on areas needing improvement.
- Talk about preassessment strategies—critical to accessing prior knowledge and to targeting instruction to areas of misunderstanding while accelerating through or reinforcing areas of mastery.
- Guide in collecting information through observation of classroom interactions, questioning, and analysis of student work.

Share strategies for prompting learner reflection and self-assessment.

- Identify strategies that engage students in reflecting on their progress and in setting personal learning goals.
- Point out opportunities for students to reflect on what they have learned and their progress as learners.
- Identify opportunities for students to develop rubrics or criteria for quality work.
- Identify appropriate points in the instruction for students to update what they are learning and to correct any misunderstandings (e.g., by summarizing key points, by refining initial understandings).
- Guide in developing a system for students to maintain their own record of progress (folders, portfolios, and checklists).

Model how to adapt assessment strategies to meet the needs of diverse learners.

- Promote an understanding of measurement theory and related issues such as validity, reliability, bias, and scoring concerns.
- Provide information about appropriate modifications for assessments (according to IEPs).
- Assist in adapting assessments to give accurate and adequate information about progress of each individual learner.

Assist in developing effective monitoring routines to detect and correct misunderstandings in a timely manner.

- Guide in using a variety of forms and sources of objective feedback to communicate progress on objectives.
- Model how to relate feedback to standards of performance including correctives and assistance to improve performance.

Provide an experienced perspective about standardized tests and constructive ways to address accountability.

- Discuss NCLB and the focus on improving the achievement of students in designated subgroups.
- Share any benchmark or required assessments as well as standardized assessments.
- Talk about the timing, purposes, formats, time limitations, etc., for these assessments.
- Collaborate to identify individual students in specific subgroups.
- Guide in identifying strategies to improve the academic performance of individuals as members of specific subgroups.
- Provide guidance in conducting an item analysis of state and classroom assessments and using previous year's test scores of current students to guide instructional planning.

PRINCIPLE 9: REFLECTION AND PROFESSIONAL DEVELOPMENT

The teacher is a reflective practitioner who continually evaluates the effects of her/his choices and actions on others (students, parents, and other professionals in the learning community) and who actively seeks out opportunities to grow professionally.

Promote realistic reflections and self-assessments that result in improved outcomes for students.

- Model methods of inquiry that provide a variety of self-assessment and problem-solving strategies for reflecting on practice and the impact of professional practice on students' growth and learning.
- Model important professional habits of mind such as critical and creative thinking and self-directed learning.
- Engage the new teacher in any schoolwide or departmental action research.

Emphasize the importance of being personally responsible for professional growth.

- Emphasize major areas of research on teaching and of resources available for professional learning (e.g., professional literature, professional associations, professional development activities, or colleagues).
- Reinforce a willingness to receive and give help and to strive to refine practices that address the individual needs of students.
- Model a constructive problem-solving approach to feedback.
- Model a commitment to personal and professional growth by personal renewal by identifying timely and relevant instructional improvement goals.
- Assist in planning the transfer of professional learning into instructional plans and classroom practice.

Promote reflection on teaching practice through careful examination of classroom evaluation and assessments.

- Engage in collaborative review of student work.
- Share assessment evidence and identify ways to adjust instruction.
- Collaborate to determine what worked and what didn't. Replanning suggestions might address pacing, remediation, needed background knowledge or prerequisite skills, enrichment, grouping, etc.

Guide reflecting on the performance of individuals and important subgroups.
- Guide in disaggregating assessment data by student subgroups or performance quintiles to identify students' strengths and needs.
- Suggest specific strategies that work with struggling students, diverse groups, or students who need enrichment and more challenge (e.g., methods and activities to accommodate the learning of *ALL* students).
- Model the planning process by first identifying students' strengths (what they know and can do), then brainstorming for possible accommodations that might address students' challenges.
- Suggest the use of audiotape, videotape, and/or a peer coach to provide detailed, objective information about classroom events and interactions (e.g., scripting or videotaping lessons and engaging in collaborative analysis).

Monitor professional growth and develop plans and experiences that will ensure positive responses from students.
- Work with the mentor team to communicate clear expectations for professional growth and performance.
- Use data and self-assessments to develop plans that build on teaching strengths and identify priorities for growth related to the teaching assignment.
- Assist in breaking long range planning into doable yet challenging steps, with periodic "due dates" for steady implementation.
- Recommend engaging in job-embedded, collegial strategies to reflect on teacher performance and student outcomes (e.g., classroom visits, examination of student work or teacher work, peer observations).
- Guide to incorporate varied experiences and formats, including but not limited to self-study, study groups, conferences, institutes, seminars, online courses, distance learning. Organize sharing of new professional learning and insights with colleagues.
- Document and share positive changes in teaching practice to reinforce efforts and accomplishments.

PRINCIPLE 10: COLLABORATION, ETHICS, AND RELATIONSHIPS

The teacher communicates and interacts with parents/guardians, families, school colleagues, and the community to support students' learning and well-being.

Provide opportunities for productive collaboration with colleagues to enhance learning for students.
- Suggest ways to contribute to collective plans with shared instructional materials.
- Facilitate departmental or grade-level sharing—and an opportunity to learn from others outside the new teacher's primary teaching assignment (e.g., curriculum generalists, technology specialists).

Communicate clearly the purpose, scope, and outcome of collaborative opportunities.
- Model commitment to collaboration for the purpose of improved student achievement.
- Assure that the new teacher understands the value of collaborative planning and assessment and how it should impact teaching and learning.

- Guide the new teacher in avoiding negative influences on collaborative practices (i.e., experienced teachers who do not perceive its value, complaints about time demands).
- Monitor the amount of time required of new teachers for collaborative work. Discourage early leadership roles to assure that new teachers have adequate time to plan for their own classroom responsibilities.

Model the importance of and ways to maintain supportive professional relationships with colleagues.

- Encourage new teachers to develop positive relationships with all faculty and staff.
- Point out the necessity of avoiding gossip or nonsupportive dialogue at all times—and in all interactions at school and outside of school.
- Consistently demonstrate respect, accessibility, and expertise when interacting with students, colleagues, parents, administrators, and stakeholders.
- Clearly communicate the need to be a "team player" and to help others out when assistance is needed.
- Provide feedback if actions or talk reflect lack of understanding, respect, or support.

Ensure implementation of laws related to students' rights and teacher responsibilities.

- Provide information about equal education, appropriate education for students with disabilities, confidentiality, privacy, appropriate treatment of students, and reporting in situations related to possible child abuse.
- Monitor understanding with questions or potential situations.

Guide in establishing respectful relationships with parents and guardians from diverse home and community situations.

- Clearly communicate the need to establish productive partnerships with parenting adults.
- Share your strategies for connecting with parents (e.g., expectations for behavior and assignments, availability to conference or assist with tutoring or additional work, ways to volunteer or assist).
- Provide introductions to individuals and agencies helpful in addressing the needs of students.

Model ways to work with parenting adults and/or community volunteers.

- Help lower new teachers' level of anxiety in working with other adults by identifying ways volunteers can be engaged productively.
- Share school policies related to volunteers, any training they receive, and the established guidelines for working productively with these adults.
- Help identify specific community volunteers or leaders who could be accessed as "speakers" or resources for specific areas of the new teacher's curriculum.
- Provide specific examples of and suggestions for effective "parent night" or "parent meetings." (Many MCTs hold seminars on this before the first "open house," "parent night," or "parent conferences.")

Guide reflection about the varied and multiple influences that impact learning in the classroom.

- Discuss the many external factors that influence learning, such as politics at the federal, state, and local levels; physical factors of the school and classroom; and parental and community expectations.

- Discuss the many internal influences that affect learning, such as the characteristics of the learners, and the teachers' knowledge of content, instructional expertise, and enthusiasm for teaching.
- Model commitment to capitalizing on the positive influences and developing strategies to overcome the negative ones.
- Guide in developing a strong sense of self-efficacy in making a difference with students.

Advise about the necessity of performing professional responsibilities efficiently and effectively.

- Provide relevant information on school policies and procedures often found in the faculty handbook.
- Model consistency in maintaining accurate and up-to-date records, completing assigned tasks on schedule, and maintaining satisfactory records of punctuality and attendance.
- Provide corrective feedback if inappropriate actions occur.

Advise about the importance of consulting with mentors and other knowledgeable educators regarding the well-being of students.

- Point out the importance of being an advocate for students, concerned about all aspects of the child's well-being (cognitive, emotional, social, and physical), and being alert to signs of difficulties.
- Monitor for understanding of actions that have legal ramifications.
- Advise about ways to maintain student privacy and confidentiality of information except when confidentiality would harm the child.
- Model the teacher's role of talking with and listening to students—being sensitive and responsive to clues of distress.
- Advise to always seek assistance from appropriate others as needed and to use caution in investigating any situation.

References and Further Readings

Alliance for Excellent Education. (2005, August). Teacher attrition: A costly loss to the nation and to the states. Washington, DC: Author.

Allington, Richard L. (2002). You can't learn much from books you can't read. *Educational Leadership, 60,* 16.

Bellon, J. J., Bellon, E. C., & Blank, M. A. (1992). *Teaching from a research knowledge base: A development and renewal process.* New York: Macmillan.

Bellon, J. J., Bellon, E. C., Blank, M. A., & Kershaw, C. A. (1992). *Observing, evaluating, and improving instruction: A professional development process.* Knoxville: The University of Tennessee.

Bellon, J. J., Bellon, E. C., Blank, M. A., & Kershaw, C. (1998). *Observing, evaluating, and improving instruction.* Unpublished manuscript.

Berliner, D. C. (1998). *Implications of studies of expertise in pedagogy for teacher education and evaluation.* Paper presented at the Educational Testing Service Invitational Conference, New York, NY.

Blank, M. A., & Kershaw, C. (1998). *The designbook for building partnerships: Home, school, and community.* Lancaster, PA: Technomic Press.

Blank, M. A., Kershaw, C. A., Russell, R., & Wright, D. (2006). *The impact of systemic induction on teacher retention and student achievement: Lessons learned from highly effective mentor-protégé pairs in schools with high implementing mentor teams in one metropolitan district.* Paper presented at the annual convention of American Educational Research Association, San Francisco, CA.

Blank, M. A., Kershaw, C., Suters, L., & Humphrey, M. (2004). *The impact of a systemic mentoring and induction program initiative.* Paper presented at the American Education Research Association, San Diego, CA.

Bloom, Benjamin. (1981). *All our children learning.* New York: McGraw-Hill.

Cochran-Smith, M. (2003, February). The unforgiving complexity of teaching: Avoiding simplicity in the age of accountability. *Journal of Teacher Education, 54*(1), 3–5.

Cohen, D. K., & Hill, H. C. (1998). *Instructional policy and classroom performance: The mathematics reform in California.* Consortium for Policy Research in Education (CPRE) Research Report Series RR-39. Philadelphia: Consortium for Policy Research in Education.

Collins, J. (2001). *Good to great: Why some companies make the leap . . . and others don't.* New York: HarperCollins Publishers Inc.

Costa, A. L., & Garmston, R. J. (1994). *Cognitive coaching: A foundation for Renaissance Schools.* Norwood, MA: Christopher-Gordon Publishers.

Cotton, K. (2000). *Research you can use to improve results.* Alexandria, VA: Association for Supervision and Curriculum Development.

Critical Friends Protocols from *Annenberg Institute for School Reform: The Consultancy: A Structured Conversation.* Retrieved [June 4, 2001] from http://www.annenberginstitute. org/tools/using_data/peer_observation/consultancy.html

Darling-Hammond, L. (1992). *Model Standards for Beginning Teacher Licensing, Assessment and Development: A Resource for State Dialogue.* Washington, DC: INTASC—A Program of the Council of Chief State School Officers.

Darling-Hammond, L. (2003, May). Keeping good teachers: Why it matters, what leaders can do. *Educational Leadership, 60*(8), 6–13.

Darling-Hammond, L., & Youngs, P. (2002). Defining "highly qualified teachers": What does "scientifically-based research" actually tell us? *Educational Researcher, 31*(9), 13–25.

Davis, G., & Metzger, M. (2006, Jan/Feb). Teachers mentoring teachers. *Edge 1*(3).

Desimone, L., Porter, A. C., & Garet, M. S. (2002). Effects of professional development on teachers' instruction: Results from a three-year longitudinal study. *Educational Evaluation and Policy Analysis, 24*(2), 81–112.

Delpit, L. (1991). *Other people's children: Cultural conflict in the classroom.* Paper presented at the 12th annual Charles H. Thompson Lecture Colloquium, Washington, DC.

DuFour, R., DuFour, R., Eaker, R., & Karhanek, G. (2004). *Whatever it takes: How professional learning communities respond when kids don't learn* (R. Dufour, Ed.). Bloomington, IN: National Educational Service.

Dweck, C. (2006). *Mindset: The new psychology of success.* New York: Random House.

Elmore, R. F. (2000, Winter). *Building a new structure for school leadership.* Washington, DC: The Albert Shanker Institute.

Feiman-Nemser, S. (2001). Mentor moves: Lessons from an exemplary mentor. *Journal of Teacher Education, 52*(1), 17–30.

Fletcher, S., & Barrett, A. (2004). Developing effective beginning teachers through mentor-based induction. *Mentoring and Tutoring, 12*(3), 321–333. Found at New Teacher Center abstracts.

Fuller, F. (1969). Concerns of teachers: A developmental conceptualization. *AER Journal, 6,* 207–226.

Garet, M. S., Porter, A. C., & Desimone, L. (2001). What makes professional development effective? Analysis of a national sample of teachers. *American Education Research Journal, 38*(4), 915–945.

Ginsberg, M. B. (2001, Spring). Data-in-a-Day technique provides a snapshot of teaching that motivates. *Journal of Staff Development, 22*(2), 1–10.

Ginsberg, M. B., & Murphy, D. (2002). How walkthroughs open doors. *Educational Leadership, 59*(8), 34–36.

Gless, J., & Moir, E. Supporting beginning teacher with heart and mind: A decade of lessons learned from the Santa Cruz New Teacher Center Project. Retrieved May, 2007, at http://www.newteachercenter.org/article7.php

Glickman, C. D. (1985). *Supervision of instruction: A developmental approach.* Boston: Allyn & Bacon.

Gordon, S. (1991). *How to help beginning teachers succeed.* Alexandria, VA: Association for Supervision and Curriculum Development.

Gray & Associates. (1985). Mentorship Training Programs, Vancouver, BC, Canada.

Grossman, P., Thompson, C., & Valencia, S. (2001, June). *District policy and beginning teachers: Where the twain shall meet.* A research report co-sponsored by Center for the Study of Teaching and Policy and National Research Center on English Learning and Achievement at the University at Albany, NY. Seattle: Center for the Study of Teaching and Policy, University of Washington.

Guskey, T. R. (2002, March). Redesigning professional development. Educational Leadership, *59*(6), 45–51.

Haycock, K. (2005, May/June). Choosing to matter more. *Journal of Teacher Education, 56*(3), 256–265.

Hord, S. M. (2007, Summer). Learn in Community with Others. *Journal of Staff Development, 28*(3), 39–40.

Howey, K. (March, 2000). *A review of challenges and innovations in the preparation of teachers for urban contexts: Implications for state policy.* Washington, DC: Office of Educational Research and Improvement.

Ingersoll, R. (2001). Teacher turnover and teacher shortages: An organizational analysis. *American Educational Research Journal, 38*(3), 499–534.

Ingersoll, R., & Kralik, J. M. (2004). *The impact of mentoring on teacher retention: What the research says.* Washington, DC: Education Commission of the States (ECS).

Ingersoll, R., & Smith, T. M. (2004). Do teacher induction and mentoring matter? *NASSP Bulletin, 88*(638), 28–40.

Interstate New Teacher Assessment and Support Consortium [INTASC]. (1992). Council of Chief State School Officers' *Model Standards for Beginning Teacher Licensing, Assessment and Development: A Resource for State Dialogue.* Washington, DC: Author.

Johnson, S. M., Kardos, S. M., Kauffman, D., Liu, E., & Donaldson, M. L. (2004, October). The support gap: New teachers' early experiences in high-income and low-income schools. *Education Policy Analysis Archives, 12*(61).

Johnston, J. M., & Ryan, K. (1980). *Research on the beginning teacher: Implications for teacher education.* ERIC Database, ED209188.

Kennedy, M. (1998). *Form and substance in inservice teacher education.* Research Monograph Number 13. Madison: National Institute for Science Education, University of Wisconsin—Madison.

Kershaw, C., Blank, M. A., Benner, S., Russell, R., Wright, D., Jackson, S., et al. (2006). *Building capacity in urban schools through teacher leadership: The Urban Specialist Certificate Program.* San Francisco, CA: A paper presented at the annual convention of the American Educational Research Association.

Killion, J. (2003). 8 smooth steps. *Journal of Staff Development, 24*(4), 14–21.

Kozol, J. (2007, Aug. 29) Letters to a young teacher: Why new recruits leave inner-city classrooms—and what it will take to keep them there. *Education Week, 27*(1), 40.

Ladson-Billings, G. (1994). *The dreamkeepers: Successful teachers of African-American children.* San Francisco, CA: Jossey-Bass.

Lambert, L. (2003). *Leadership capacity: For lasting school improvement.* Alexandria, VA: Association for Supervision and Curriculum Development.

Langer, G. M., Colton, A. B., & Goff, L. S. (2003). *Collaborative analysis of student work: Improving teaching and learning.* Alexandria, VA: Association for Supervision and Curriculum Development.

Likert, R. (1967). *Human organization: Its management and value.* New York: McGraw-Hill.

Marzano, R. J. (2007). *The art and science of teaching: A comprehensive framework for effective instruction.* Alexandria, VA: Association for Supervision and Curriculum Development.

Marzano, R. J., Pickering, D. J., & Pollack, J. E. (2001). *Classroom instruction that works: Research-based strategies for increasing student achievement.* Alexandria, VA: Association for Supervision and Curriculum Development.

Marzano, R. J., Pickering, D. J., Arredondo, D. E., Blackburn, G.J., Brandt, R. S., Moffett, C. A., et al. (1997). *Dimensions of learning.* Alexandria, VA: Association for Supervision and Curriculum Development.

Marzano, R. J., Pickering, D. J., Arredondo, D. E., Blackburn, G. J., Brandt, R. S., Moffett, C.A., et al. (1997). *Dimensions of learning: Teacher's manual.* Alexandria, VA: Association for Supervision and Curriculum Development.

Mayer, D. P., Mullens, J. E., Moore, M. T., & Ralph, J. (2000). *Monitoring school quality: An indicators report.* Washington, DC: National Center for Education Statistics, Office of Educational Research and Improvement, U.S. Department of Education.

McLaughlin, M. W., & Talbert, J. E. (1993). *Contexts that matter for teaching and learning: Strategic opportunities for meeting the nation's education goals.* Stanford, CA: Center for Research on the Context of Secondary School Teaching, Stanford University.

Moir, E., & Bloom, G. (May 2003). Fostering leadership through mentoring. *Educational Leadership, 60*(8), 58–60.

National Education Association [NEA]. (2004, June). *Teacher quality: Moving forward.* A dialogue with The Teaching Commission Teaching at Risk: A call to action. Washington, DC: Author.

NEA Foundation for the Improvement of Education. (2002, Summer). Using data to improve teacher induction programs. (Issue Brief No. 4). Washington, DC: Author.

Northwest Regional Educational Laboratory. (2005). Fast Facts: What are PLTs? Retrieved [AUTHOR; June, 2004] from www.nwrel.org/scpd/sslc/institutes_2005/documents/abel_plt_fast_facts.pdf

Perkins, E., & Hu, T. (2007, January). Intergenerational workforce (Impact of aging and intergenerational workforce). Presentation to AAIA Career Workshop: IEEE-USA Career and Workforce Policy Committee. Retrieved November 11, 2007 from (www.aiaa.org/pdf/myaiaa/workshop/Intergenerational_Workforce_AIAA07.pdf)

Roberts, S. & Pruitt, E. (2003). *Schools as professional learning communities.* Thousand Oaks, CA: Corwin Press.

Rosenholtz, S. (1989). *Teachers' workplace: The social organization of schools.* New York: Longman.

Rowley, J. B. (2000). *High-performance mentoring.* Thousand Oaks, CA: Corwin Press.

Sagor, R. (2003). *Motivating students and teachers in an era of standards.* Alexandria, VA: Association for Supervision and Curriculum Development.

Sanders, W. L. (2000). Value-added assessment from student achievement data: Opportunities and hurdles. *Journal of Personnel Evaluation in Education, 14*(4), 329–339.

Sanders, W. L., & Horn, S. P. (1998). Research findings from the Tennessee value-added assessment system (TVAAS) database: Implications for educational evaluation and research. *Journal of Personnel Evaluation in Education, 12,* 247–256.

Schmoker, M. (1999). *Results: The key to continuous school improvement (2nd ed).* Alexandria, VA: Association for Supervision and Curriculum Development.

Schmoker, M. (2004, February). Tipping point: From feckless reform to substantive instructional improvement. *Phi Delta Kappan, 85*(6), 424–432.

Schmoker, M. (2006). *Results now: How we can achieve unprecedented improvements in teaching and learning.* Alexandria, VA: Association for Supervision and Curriculum Development.

Smylie, M. A., Allensworth, E., Greenberg, R. C., Harris, R., & Luppescu, S. (2001). *Teacher professional development in Chicago: Supporting effective practice.* Report of the Chicago Annenburg Research Project. Chicago: Consortium on Chicago School Research.

Sparks, D. (2002, December) High-performing cultures increase teacher retention, National Staff Development Council. Retrieved July 10, 2007, from National Staff Development Council Web site: http://www.nsdc.org/library/publications/results/res12-02spar.cfm

Stiggens, R. (1997). *Student-centered classroom assessment.* Upper Saddle River, NJ: Prentice Hall.

Strong, M., Fletcher, S., & Villar, A. (2004). *An investigation of the effects of teacher experiences and teacher preparedness on the performance of Latino students in California.* Santa Cruz, CA: New Teacher Center.

Strong, R. W., Silver, H. F., & Perini, M. J. (2001). *Teaching what matters most: Standards and strategies for raising student achievement.* Alexandria, VA: Association for Supervision and Curriculum Development.

Treadway, L. (2000). *Community mapping.* Unpublished manuscript prepared for Contextual Teaching and Learning Project, The Ohio State University, and U.S. Department of Education.

Villani, S. (2004). Building a framework: Induction and mentoring programs that work. In *Keeping quality teachers: The art of retaining general and special education teachers,* (pp. 4.1–4.47). New York, NY: New York State Education Department.

Villar, A. (2005). *Is mentoring worth the money? A benefit-cost analysis and five-year rate of return of a comprehensive mentoring program for beginning gteachers.* Manuscript submitted for publication.

Weiner, L. (1999). *Urban teaching: The essentials.* New York: Teachers' College Press.

Wenglinsky, H. (2000). *How teaching matters: Bringing the classroom back into discussions of teacher quality.* Princeton, NJ: Policy Information Center of the Educational Testing Service and the Milken Family Foundation.

Wiggins, G. (1998). *Educative assessment: Designing assessments to inform and improve performance.* San Francisco: Jossey-Bass.

Wiggins, G., & McTighe, J. (1998). *Understanding by design.* Arlington, VA: Association for Supervision and Curriculum Development.

Williams, B. (Ed.). (1996). *Closing the achievement gap: A vision for changing beliefs and practices.* Alexandria, VA: Association for Supervision and Curriculum Development.

Wong, H. K. (2001, August 8). Mentoring can't do it all. *Education Week, 20*(43), 46, 50.

Young, L. J. (1998). Culturally relevant pedagogy in contextual teaching and learning. In S. J. Sears & S. Hersh (Eds.), *Contextual teaching and learning: Preparing teachers to enhance student success in the workplace and beyond.* Columbus, OH: Urban Network to Improve Teacher Education.

Zemke, R., Raines, C., & Flipczak, R. (2000). *Generations at work: Managing the clash of veterans, boomers, Xers and Nexters in your workplace.* New York: Amacom.

Zimmerman, J., & Stansbury, K. (2000). *Lifelines to the classroom: Designing support for beginning teachers.* (WestEd Knowledge Brief.) Retrieved May 2005 from http://www.wested.org/cs/we/view/rs/212

Index

The Corwin Press logo—a raven striding across an open book—represents the union of courage and learning. Corwin Press is committed to improving education for all learners by publishing books and other professional development resources for those serving the field of PreK–12 education. By providing practical, hands-on materials, Corwin Press continues to carry out the promise of its motto: **"Helping Educators Do Their Work Better."**